MW00604295

PASS THE BUSINESS,
Please.

How to Transition
the Family Company
to the Next Generation

LOIS LANG, Psy.D.

Pass the Business, Please: How to Transition the Family Company to the Next Generation

Copyright © 2013 by Lois Lang, Psy.D. All Rights Reserved

www.evolvepartnergroup.com

No part of this publication may be reproduced or transmitted in any form or by any means, mechanical or electronic, including photocopying and recording, or by any information storage and retrieval system, without permission in writing from author or publisher (except by a reviewer, who may quote brief passages and/or show brief video clips in a review). Disclaimer: The Publisher and the Author make no representations or warranties with respect to the accuracy or completeness of the contents of this work and specially disclaim all warranties, including without limitation warranties of fitness for a particular purpose. No warranty may be created or extended by sales or promotional materials. The advice and strategies contained herein may not be suitable for every situation. This work is sold with the understanding that the Publisher is not engaged in rendering legal, accounting, or other professional services. If professional assistance is required, the services of a competent professional person should be sought. Neither the Publisher nor the Author shall be liable for damages arising here from. The fact that an organization or website is referred to in this work as a citation and/or a potential source of further information does not mean that the Author or the Publisher endorses the information the organization or website may provide or recommendations it may make. Further, readers should be aware that internet websites listed in this work may have changed or disappeared between when this work was written and when it is read.

ISBN: 978-0-9889110-0-0

Printed in the United States of America

2013

DEDICATION

To my family, Roger, Amy, Chris, Ella, Andrew, Milos, Bryan, Michael, Julie, and Lucas.

And to my original family, Mom, Dad, Glenn, Nancy, Daniel, Michael, Beth, Kyri, and Paul.

I am richly blessed.

ACKNOWLEDGEMENTS

The level of gratitude I feel to the number of people who have assisted me on this journey is hard to describe.

Thank you to both the family members and employees of La Tortilla Factory, Lundberg Family Farms, and "Interiors Unlimited." You were all very open with my endless questions and welcomed me into your businesses and homes. I am indebted.

Thank you to Dawn Josephson, my awesome development writing coach and editor. I couldn't have completed this without your expertise, support, and not-so-gentle nudges. I'd like to also give a shout out to my other editor, Katy Berry, who now has her sights set on being a screenwriter.

To my colleagues Larry Hansen, Matt Page, CFP®, and Michael Sollazzo, Esq., at Capital Planning Advisors, Inc. in Sacramento, CA, thank you for your technical expertise. You have always taken great care of my clients, and have kept me on target with the latest and best strategies for the accumulation and preservation of wealth. Thank you, gentlemen!

To Kara Menghini, thank you for the endless support you've always provided. Throughout this whole process you've made sure my clients were well cared for, left me space for writing, and prodded me when I needed it. Thank you also to my business partner, Cathy Gibson, for your support and understanding that time squirreled away writing will ultimately positively impact what we can bring to our clients' succession work. I am fortunate to be surrounded by you two strong, successful business women.

Thank you to Hal Johnson and Kurt Glassman at LeadershipOne. None of this could have happened if I hadn't had competent and tireless mentoring from you. You introduced me to the fascinating world of families in business, and I will always be grateful for that. You are both professional, caring, and open—a rare combination.

And of course, thank you to my husband, Roger. I know you probably enjoyed some of the extra fishing trips you took this year while I was cemented to my desk writing. Even so, you never complained about my writing schedule, and you dutifully brought me tea and listened to my incessant rambling. I couldn't have done this without your support. Finally, a special thank you to my children and grandchildren. I know you have seen less of me during this process. Even so, we have managed to stay connected. You are what brings joy to my life.

CONTENTS

INTRODUCTION

We've all heard family business survival statistics with varying numbers, but the overall storyline is the same: The ability for a family-owned business to survive through the third generation is unlikely. One recent data source[1] concluded that the level of entrepreneurial drive, risk, and innovation orientations of these families led to their demise.

The rule of 30-13-3 percent was originally introduced by John Ward in 1987 and is still widely accepted. His study found that 30 percent of family-owned businesses survive through the second generation, 13 percent survive through the third generation, and only 3 percent survive beyond that.

These statistics are frequently used to bring up fear for families in business, yet in 2001, Aronoff[2] found that survival rates of publicly traded, non-family businesses were not significantly better. As such, the positive side of family business has the potential to far outweigh this doom and gloom, if the family takes a long-term perspective and actively plans.

While many of the businesses I have worked with haven't made it through the third generation, I began reflecting on the businesses I've known that were flourishing into the third, fourth and fifth generations.

1   Zellweger, Thomas, Nason, Robert and Nordqvist, Mattias, "From Longevity of Firms to Transgenerational Entrepreneurship of Families: Introducing Family Entrepreneurial Orientation." *Family Business Review,* November 2011, Sage Publications.

2   University of St. Gallen, St. Gallen, Switzerland

I then compared them to businesses that hobbled along in the first generation and crumbled during their transition into the second.

During my analysis, I identified four key areas that support transition. They are:

1. A healthy family

2. A commitment to talent development

3. Good governance

4. On-going planning

In addition to offering perspective on these four areas, this book also gives an inside look at three family business transitions, two of which make it to the next generation; one business sprints, the other walks, and the third one explodes before arrival.

If the current leadership of your family business is committed to getting the company to the next generation, it is my hope that you will find a perspective here that stimulates you and your family to action.

"Feelings of worth can flourish only in an atmosphere where individual differences are appreciated, mistakes are tolerated, communication is open, and rules are flexible—the kind of atmosphere that is found in a nurturing family."
–VIRGINIA SATIR

CHAPTER 1

THE FAMILIES AT THE TABLE

You love your family and you know your business, so why are you pulling out your hair or rubbing your bald head to a shine? Dealing with family relationships, especially within an increasingly complex business environment, is an intense, personal, and often overwhelming endeavor.

No matter what you're going through right now with your family business, rest assured that you're not alone. Throughout this book you will meet and learn about three different family businesses. Through their stories, along with my narrative and perspective, you will better understand the four keys to a successful transition of the business to the next generation.

The four keys we'll be focusing on are:

1. A Healthy Family

2. Commitment to Talent Development

3. Good Governance

4. On-Going Planning

The Families

Let's start with the three CEOs who will serve as our examples throughout the book. First, there is Carlos Tamayo, past CEO and present Chairman of the Board of La Tortilla Factory.

La Tortilla Factory

Carlos personifies La Tortilla Factory. Standing at five foot, eight inches, he is clearly of Hispanic descent, from his warm chocolate complexion, dark hair, and brown eyes to his thick graying moustache. Fit, trim, and handsome, he reflects his and the business' dedication to a healthy lifestyle. His smile floods his face and makes you respond in kind. While personally driven, he is often described by employees as easy-going and inclusive—casually walking the halls and production floor inquiring about the product and family of employees in a sincere, seamless manner. His office has beautiful bright, warm colors and original watercolors offset by his grandchildren's crayon drawings; books are predominant and plentiful.

Carlos's parents, Jose Tamayo (born in 1924) and Mary Rita Vieyra (born in 1918), knew the meaning of perseverance and hard work. Jose worked odd jobs in Mexico where he was the fourth oldest of 12 children, quitting school at the age of 12 to help support the family. Jose came to America during World War II through the U.S. government's Bracero program and became a naturalized citizen. He was proud of his contributions in support of the war effort as a railroader keeping the trains moving. Mary was a first generation Mexican American who worked as a farm worker in the beet fields with her parents throughout the Midwest. Mary's biggest regret was that her mother forced her to quit high school a few months before graduation, believing that it was unnecessary for women, especially Latino women. As a result, she dedicated herself to ensuring that her children would receive a college education. They met and married in North Platte, Nebraska in 1944, where both Jose and Mary's brothers were working at Union Pacific Railroad.

Jose and Mary had five sons—Carlos, Jose de Jesus (Tico), Willie, Bernie, and Mike. They moved from North Platte to Omaha, Nebraska in search of a better education for their children; later, they were proud that all five of their sons graduated from college.

Carlos had graduated from college and was working at a bank when his father became unemployed after 30 years with the railroad. Carlos began looking for businesses his father could run, including a liquor store and forest contracts. Neither of these businesses appealed to Jose, and after further research Carlos suggested tortilla production.

Willie Tamayo, Andy Tamayo, Sam Tamayo, Carlos Tamayo (standing left to right); Jose Tamayo (sitting)

Jose agreed and went to work for six months in a tortilla factory to better understand the business. In 1977, Jose and Mary moved from Omaha to Santa Rosa, California to start producing tortillas and running a deli and fast food Mexican restaurant. They provided the initial capitalization of the business from series E Bonds that they purchased every two weeks throughout their marriage. Tico, Carlos, and Willie also added money to round out their parents' contribution and the Small Business Administration loan. Carlos traded in his personal car for a delivery van.

When Carlos talks about the way it started he says:

"The way I tell the story is that God places dreams in the minds of visionary people. There was no doubt that my father was visionary. My mother was, too, but she bought into his dream. It was always talked about, mentioned to us as kids. That dream was to start a business."

While the family's primary business was the restaurant, they soon found that they had to "sell a lot of burritos" to simply cover the rent. The beginning years were a struggle—long hours, six and seven days a week. Carlos and his younger brother Willie were primarily in the business with their father, Jose, but everyone chipped in. Bernie and Tico often worked on the weekends so Carlos and Willie could take off one day a week. Mike worked during high school breaks and joined soon after graduating from college.

Carlos was the general organizer and operational guy; Willie soon landed in sales as he proved to be a natural, and Mike worked in product

development. Carlos noted that, "It was difficult pulling us all together... we are all strong-willed people who were taught to be driven and independent [by our parents]. My mother couldn't get us to do what she wanted, so I'm not sure how I thought I could do it."

The La Tortilla Employee Team

While the restaurant was their main focus, they were also running a small deli/general store and producing tortillas to sell to local businesses. As Carlos said, "We sold anything that would bring in money—piñatas, tortillas, hot sauce."

Carlos has faced several challenges along the way to success: First was the challenge of working long hard hours, yet not growing the business enough to financially sustain the extended family. Second was deciding whether he wanted the business as an asset to develop and sell, or as a legacy business to honor their parents for the great sacrifices they made to start the family business and pass it on to subsequent generations. Third, he struggled with choosing his successor and the greater challenge of releasing some control of the business. In the midst of this, Carlos experienced a crisis and renewal of his spirituality. Carlos' message is that if you persevere, seek advice, gather knowledge, release personal control, and have faith in God, you will succeed.

Lundberg Family Farms

Grant's build and demeanor portray that of Socratic thought, inclusion, and care of the land. Standing at 6 foot 3 inches, he is slight, with ash blonde, gently curling shoulder length hair, intense blue eyes, thin nose; frequently dressed in jeans and a sports jacket. He exemplifies the concept of servant leader with specific answers that point to the team and family effort that support his leadership at Lundberg. He is quick to point out their tireless determination to match quality products with best business practices, coupled with a high value placed on talent, both family and non-family.

Grant Lundberg[3]

Grant had excellent role models from the era of his father, uncles, and grandfather. He is noted for being an astute business leader and skilled at family inclusion. When he took the CEO role in 1998, he had 14 direct reports and was challenged to strategically lead a large diverse group. In 2004, the Board, after several months of conversation, agreed to his restructuring that prepared them for further growth.

Lundberg Family Farms began in 1937 when Albert and Frances Lundberg moved from Nebraska to California after the devastating dustbowl. They settled in the small town of Richvale in the Sacramento Valley. Albert's experience with Nebraska's poor soil management and farming practices (leading to the destructive Dustbowl) led him to value the care of the land. He was a pioneer in organic rice growing in America. Lundberg Family Farms is now the nation's leading producer of organic rice and rice products.

Albert and Frances' four sons, Eldon, Wendell, Harlan, and Homer, began selling rice directly to the public in the 1960s, beginning the Lundberg Family Farms® brand of quality rice products. Eldon and

3   Courtesy of California Rice Commission and photographer, Paulo Vescia.

Ruth had three children: Jennifer (born in 1957), Grant (born in 1963), and Julianne (born in 1964). Grant is currently the Chief Executive Officer.

Eldon retired from daily management of the family business in 1999, beginning the transition to the third generation of Lundberg family rice farmers. Eldon passed away in June 2010 at age 82.

Wendell J. Lundberg, the second of the four brothers, was born August 17, 1930. Wendell was an airplane pilot like his brother Eldon, and an ardent world traveler. He managed a rice experiment in Australia and on his return in 1955, began farming with his father and brothers. Wendell married Carolyn Osborn in 1971 and had three children: Joe, Jessica and Alysicia. Jessica was the Chairperson of the Board and now serves as the Vice President of People, Planet, and Process within the business. Joe Lundberg serves as Alternative Markets Manager. Wendell phased out of the day-to-day operations in the mid 2000s. He continued as an advocate for sustainable agriculture and supporter of many local organizations and charitable causes.

Harlan Lundberg, Wendell Lundberg, Eldon Lundberg, Homer Lundberg

Harlan served in the US Army. He completed his service in 1954 and returned to farm with his brothers, Eldon, Wendell, and Homer. Harlan and his wife, Carolyn, were married for more than 50 years and in addition to their three sons, Mark, Bryce, and Eric, they were foster parents to dozens of children. Bryce currently serves as Vice President of Agriculture in the family business. Harlan was instrumental in the adoption of organic and eco-friendly farming practices. His interest extended to the development of new rice varieties and the production of rice cakes and other rice-based products. Harlan, like his brothers, was actively engaged in industry, community, church, and charity activities. Harlan passed away in August 2011 at the age of 77.

The youngest brother, Homer, was born in Nebraska, moving with his parents to California when he was just two. He attended Yuba College and California State University, Fresno earning a Bachelor of Science degree in Agricultural Education. He joined the family business in 1959 after service in the U.S. Air Force. He married Carol Van Dyke, a third-generation California rice farmer from Pleasant Grove in 1961, and has two children, Ingrid and Kent. With his brothers, Homer started milling their own organic brown rice and selling it directly to the public in 1969. Homer served as the company's Treasurer, then Chairman. He turned this over to the next generation in 2006. Homer is a strong and vocal champion for water resources stewardship and sustainable farming practices throughout the rice industry.

Lundberg Family Farms grows, mills, processes, and packs their rice and rice products. They control the product from greenhouse to warehouse to ensure quality, taste, and care. They have a dryer, mill, rice product processing facility, and warehouse.

Lundberg Family Farms Headquarters-Richvale, California

Today, they have an elegant facility that is LEED (Leadership in Energy & Environmental Design) qualified. The building has a creative modern barn shape with a steel roof. Pulling into the front of their building, you begin to already experience their dedication to the earth, product innovation, and detail with the display of small labeled plots of different rice varieties. Inside, the ceilings are high and lofty. The lobby hosts an inviting, low circular counter and a bronze sculpture of geese over a water feature. Throughout the building, there are inviting areas for employees, visitors, and vendors to sit, mingle, and congregate. Workspaces are open with walls that bid playful writing for impromptu meetings and daily task reminders. The table in the boardroom is made from wood from the original rice dryer. Solar panels and sky lights ensure a well-lighted, airy feel while saving energy and upholding their original roots of care for the environment. The rustic tie to the past is balanced with high tech connection throughout.

Interiors Unlimited[4]

Tom's booming voice and easy-going smile are the first things you notice. He has wide shoulders, thick dark hair, a moustache, and intense brown eyes. His broad hands and deeply tanned skin hint at the long years on-site looking at draft drawings, managing job sites, and doing manual labor. While that is far in the background now, he knows how to manage from the leadership level in the office to estimates in the field, whether it's for wall coverings, ceilings, molding, cabinets, or countertops—he can do it all.

Tom's story is one of struggle, both professionally and personally. Yet it is also one of triumph. Tom is the current CEO of Interiors Unlimited; his father, Neal, was CEO until 2011. Unfortunately, Neal has worked at tearing Tom down rather than building him up.

Tom worked long hours with his father during summers and on college vacations. Neal, overwhelmed with work, convinced Tom to quit college and help out at the family business. Neal taught him all of the things to do in business, from marginal accounting practices to developing abysmal relationships with both employees and family members.

Tom hit two large turning points, one when he decided to become clean and sober, and the second when he began taking the growth of the company into his own hands. Tom, against his father's wishes, formed an instrumental and critical relationship with Corian, becoming their sole distributor on the west coast. Finally, Tom persevered during his father's succession plan, making a complete break with the family.

---

4   The name of the company, people, and type of industry has been changed, because of the current family relationships.

Tom credits a lot of his strength and ability to lead from the skills he has gained from Alcoholics Anonymous (AA). He also dug down and pulled that will power out again when he had to face his father and stepbrother for control of the business during Neal's succession. The process was embroiled in anger, demands, and deception. Tom was working sixty to seventy hours per week, stacked up by his father's gradual decline to twenty hours and his stepbrother's ineffective thirty hours a week. The business succession from one generation to the next finally deteriorated into a legal battle, and a forced receivership by the courts, before complete control was handed to Tom.

Tom now has the loyalty and respect of the employees, vendors, and customers. The best part is that he now has some work-life balance, and his daughter is quickly becoming his right hand person in the company.

Each of these individuals, Carlos at La Tortilla Factory, Grant at Lundberg Family Farms, and Tom at Interiors Unlimited, have relied deeply on their values and beliefs to carry and guide them through the transition of their family business from one generation to the next. So let's start there by looking at how values and beliefs impact the family business.

The Salt at the Table

Salt is a universal compound that is essential to life and probably the first seasoning known to man. In a way, salt is essential for human existence, since without it our bodies would not maintain the proper balance of body fluids. While salt helps keep our physical bodies in balance, our values and beliefs work together to keep our emotional and relational selves in balance. In fact, human existence is immersed in our values and beliefs. The other core ingredients of the family include the level of respect, trust, and transparency. Without this mixture, the family harmony is out of balance, and the business's sustainability falters.

Values and Beliefs

Your business reflects the strength of your family's values and beliefs. If your family believes in open dialogue and personal growth, then the business will promote transparent, on-going dialogue and support for individual employee development. Likewise, if your family has a strong belief in and practice of honesty and integrity, the business will reflect that.

For example, during an internal financial audit, one of my family business clients noted that a buyer overpaid them $20,000 during a year that was a roller coaster of feast and famine for the company, with more famine than feast. They could have easily overlooked this "error," but the family member working in the accounting department presented her findings to the CEO, her uncle, and the overpayment was promptly returned to the buyer.

Unexamined belief systems can have a negative impact on the family business. While a first generation owner's practice of high business risk, low compensation, and avoidance of a reporting structure generally works well during the start-up phase, holding onto these beliefs can jeopardize the business's sustainability into the next generation.

If you really want to throw your family and employees a good time, state one value and act differently. This will leave people confused, distrustful, angry, and resentful. As a result, you will see inconsistent employee behavior and experience low employee morale. If a family CEO states that all employees are compensated equally, but non-family employees find out that the CEO's daughter is making thirty percent more than her position warrants, it will quickly lead to resentment. It would be better for the CEO to acknowledge that family and non-family employees receive different compensation, rather than to state equality and practice inequality. Yes, I understand this isn't a legal practice; it nevertheless is a reality in many family businesses.

Carlos at La Tortilla Factory places a high value on family and on including everyone in discussions. This is reflected in the way the company makes collaborative, consensus-driven decisions. They have frequent meetings to ensure that everyone is heard and that the best ideas are surfaced. Another value they hold is respect of others; employees talk passionately about being a part of the Tamayo extended family, and Carlos is quick to thank others and show sincere appreciation.

Likewise, the values of Lundberg Family Farms are clear and in alignment with their behavior. Their values of integrity, respect, continuous improvement, and teamwork are visible in interactions between employees. The family reinforces these values in the way they treat each other, employees, vendors, customers, and the community. They state that "appreciation, gratitude, and graciousness have been fundamental traits exhibited by our family for generations, and we believe these are a key to achieving the respect we wish to characterize our company in the future." Brita Lundberg noted that her great-grandpa Albert took his philosophy of "leaving the land better than you found it" and expanded it into all parts of his life by serving others.[5]

In contrast, it's evident that Neal, as the long-term past CEO and owner of Interiors Unlimited, valued primarily himself, personal power, and money. He believed that he needed to make all of the decisions, tightly control employees, and intensely monitor his family. When it came to beliefs and values surrounding money, Neal believed that more, at all cost, was the goal. Fortunately, the values of his son Tom, the current CEO and owner, are opposite of his father's. While Tom is running the business for bottom-line value to sustain into the next generation, he encourages employee involvement, his family's input, honesty, and integrity.

The strength and consistency of the way the Tamayos and the Lundbergs treat family members have clearly carried over into their businesses, resulting in loyal and engaged employees. On the other hand, Interiors Unlimited past values of self before others, control, power, and money led to its downward spiral.

What are the values and beliefs of your family business? What things, for better or for worse, are guiding your family and business activities? If you're unsure, sit down with your family members and have the discussion. Have everyone make a list of what each perceives the family's values and beliefs to be, and then analyze the business to see if they are reflected in employee behavior. If you identify some negative or conflicting values, make a plan to change course.

---

5   Family Business Magazine, July 2012.

Respect, Trust, and Transparency

Respectful relationships within the family will lead to healthy relationships between employees. Respect is reinforced when you acknowledge others' abilities and accomplishments in the form of public praise, recognition, and competitive compensation. Let's face it, mean people gobble up workplace energy, and a bully at home will most certainly play the bully at work. The frequency of bad behavior seems to be more prominent in family businesses, where there is a relaxed sense of being able to "be ourselves" around other family members. I have even heard it excused as "he is just being honest and direct" while turnover increases and morale drops. In contrast, I was recently at a Family Council meeting where a wise CEO demanded that family employees act respectfully and work harder than non-family employees.

A high level of trust, respect, and transparency in your founding family will organically spread into the business and subsequent generations. Trust energizes a work environment. Stephen Covey, in his book *The Speed of Trust: The One Thing that Changes Everything*, details how high trust between individuals leads to quick results, high employee performance, and bottom-line company value. The more I trust that you will follow through on your word, the more likely I will enthusiastically participate in driving toward business goals.

Transparency leads to a deeper level of trust between individuals. When you are honest about what is happening in the family unit, opening up to show your vulnerability and struggle, you become more human. When you and your spouse are upset and calmly talk about it, without blaming or verbally attacking each other, you show that people can disagree and still love and support each other. This does not mean that parents should discuss personal, intimate, or hurtful details in front of their children, but that they should not hide all of life's disappointments and pain. Transparency in companies is usually seen as one department being open about their projects, deliverable schedules, and budgets so that other departments and teams can adjust and interact with them in a supportive way.

The Cervantes Distribution company, led by Raul Cervantes[6], was a third generation grocery distributor. Raul never discussed finances with his wife, Maria. He alone balanced their personal bank statements, paid the bills, and decided on their investments. Whenever Maria needed money she would ask for it.

Raul handled the business in the same way with managers who were unaware of their budgets. As the company grew, Raul would become angry that projects were frequently over budget, but he still refused to share financial information broadly. The executive management team eventually convinced him that this level of transparency was necessary for growth. As managers became accountable for their budgets, Raul noticed that not only did he reap the rewards of a healthier bottom-line, but that he also had employees that were more engaged in problem-solving and teamwork to reach goals.

La Tortilla Factory

Carlos holds a high level of trust and respect within his family that is reflected in the business. He is transparent about his drive to succeed, balanced with his belief in the potential of people. He thinks out loud, including others in his internal conversations, and is broadly transparent about successes and failures. While Carlos' control of the company has resulted in his brothers Willie and Mike feeling that they could not trust him to "give them their fair share," Carlos acknowledges that he had a control issue and has worked on it, and he has made the changes to shift control to others. He has also come to peace with loosening control on the purse strings, recognizing that they all had years of underpaid service. Both Willie and Carlos talk respectfully about each other's different strengths in sales and leadership respectively. A full employee survey that was conducted in both Spanish and English rated trust in La Tortilla Factory at a healthy rating of 3.6 out of 5, with 5 being the highest level of trust.

---

6   Based on actual client; industry and names changed.

Lundberg Family Farms

As with most family businesses, the transition from one generation to the next brings greater transparency if sustainability is valued. Lundberg, in the beginning of their fourth generation family member integration, has a Board of Directors monitoring financials, an internal department budgeting process, and openness about processes and procedures. The relationships between employees, both family and non-family, are generally respectful and collaborative, and inclusive team processes are encouraged.

Interiors Unlimited

Tom watched his dad, Neal, treat others with disrespect, trusting no one and revealing little of the business, except to his external attorney and accountant. The front office personnel were referred to as "the girls," even though many of them were well into their forties and fifties. Fault finding was common; praise rare. Neal didn't trust employees, going to great lengths to control and monitor their activities. Employees resented Neal's control and found ways to limit their productivity and harm the company. When Neal began GPS tracking company trucks, employees would go to a job site one or two hours earlier than they needed to, sleep in the truck, and charge Interiors Unlimited for the time. Other employees mapped out the longest possible way to get to the job site, taking a leisurely drive to ensure that Neal got back what he dished out. There were on-going rumors of inventory "leaving" the building and gas being pumped for personal use. There was no sense of loyalty or mutual respect between employees and owner. Tom was constantly "cleaning up my dad's mistakes" created by poor treatment of employees.

Transparency was not in Neal's vocabulary. Instead, Neal hid information from everyone, including his family. He kept and doctored books, pushed back on the corporate attorney and accountant advice, and artfully played a shell game in all of his relationships. He had a convoluted method of paying his son and stepson a base salary, and then at year-end he used an unknown formula to determine a bonus that was a large part of their income, and that sometimes disappeared back into the company before being distributed.

The respect, trust, and transparency demonstrated at both La Tortilla Factory and Lundberg Family Farms has served them well; the lack of respect, trust, and transparency at Interiors Unlimited was at the heart of their demise.

* * * * *

At the end of each chapter, you will find questions that will help you and your family reflect together and begin identifying areas to celebrate and areas to work on.

Questions for Chapter 1 – The Families at the Table:

1. What top five values does your family hold?

2. Are those family values reflected in your business?

3. How would you describe the level of trust and respect between family members?

4. What level of transparency do you have within your family?

5. What is the level of transparency within the business?

"Even the most ordinary things can be made extraordinary simply by doing it with the right people."

—NICHOLAS SPARKS

CHAPTER 2
THE GET-ALONG FACTOR

Relationships and Communication

Your ability to get along with other family members and employees will directly and positively affect your business. A leader attitude of "service to others" will trump the "I am great" attitude every day. It's hard for people to line up in admiration of a person focused on his or her own personal gain. A CEO with a mean streak will damage family relationships, negatively infect the work environment, and seep into the next generation ... if any of them stick around for that kind of fun.

While we may be taught by our parents to get along with others, that may mean different things depending on the family. For some, it's *"I need to just suck it up, be quiet, and keep going,"* while others have learned to push back, argue, debate, or influence. Few families learn how to effectively communicate unless they have had a family crisis with outside intervention requiring it. In fact, many people do not go through this type of interpersonal development except for minimal training in the workplace.

As you are open to one another and maintain an on-going, honest dialogue, you will notice these same communication patterns in the business. Being able to challenge each other, face reality together, and discuss different ideas without taking them personally carries a high bottom-line value. The *Get-Along Factor* asks everyone to be willing to disagree while supporting and respecting each other.

On the Same Page – Motive & Intention

Your commitment to getting along is bolstered by a common mission and compelling vision that is valued above individual motives and intentions. No doubt you have noticed that the *Get-Along Factor* becomes progressively more difficult from one generation to the next. Initially, a solo founding owner will only need to influence their spouse.

This scenario becomes increasingly challenged if the founding owner has one or multiple business partners, either a sibling, aunt, uncle, or non-family member. As the second generation siblings enter the business, more frequent communication needs to occur to ensure that everyone is on the same page.

Let's say that these three siblings then marry; their spouses bring three more family groups into the business. It's easy to see how the vision, motives, and intentions for the business can quickly deteriorate. Creating structured opportunities for open and frequent dialogue will serve you well.

The second generation (the owner's children) have the advantage of being raised in the same house as their parents, observing and integrating their values and communication patterns. By the third generation, cousins have been raised in different households, have heard different perspectives of the business, and are primed to have diverse opinions and visions of where the business should head. At this point, there may also be one or more divorces and introductions of even more family groups. The fun has begun!

The United Front

Similar to a mother and father who are clear and in lock step with their expectations of their children, a united family in the workplace strengthens the business. Employees feel secure in this environment, because there is a sense of comfort in knowing that the family gets along, is united in their approach, and is looking out for the best interest of the business.

The *Get-Along Factor* for the next generation rests largely on the previous generation. If the relationships between the founding siblings are healthy and strong, the next generation will likely inherit their values, beliefs, and communication style. On the other hand, troubled relationships, addiction, or divorce will bring upheaval in the family and into the business. Even with successful third and fourth generation businesses, a divorce of one family can lead to a sudden need to liquidate stock.

La Tortilla Factory

The *Get-Along Factor* at La Tortilla Factory is strong; not perfect. The five brothers were all very much determined individuals, yet a strong sense of camaraderie and loyalty to each other developed in the early years of the business. This weakened when Mike, the youngest brother, decided to exercise the buy-sell agreement and leave the company in 2007 to start his own business. Carlos and Willie were supportive and worked hard to be fair in order to maintain good family relationships. They both thanked him for his many contributions over the years to the success of the business. In 2008, Carlos and Willie executed their management succession plan and Carlos transitioned to Chairman of the Board, while Stan Mead, the non-family CFO, assumed the CEO position. Carlos and Willie still work together in the company. And although Carlos has continued to make attempts to give ample opportunity for other family members from other branches to participate and grow into future leadership drivers, as commonly happens, the business is becoming primarily driven by one branch of the family.

Focus groups of employees consistently rate the Tamayo family and La Tortilla Factory as effectively creating a work environment that is open, communicative, challenging, inclusive, and friendly; employee focus group dialogue also revealed that they view themselves as a family of employees within a progressive family business. Employees not only feel like a part of the Tamayo family, but many of them have their own family members working within the company and are encouraged to introduce family members and friends to La Tortilla Factory employment if they feel they would be a fit to the culture—willing to learn, loyal, and hard working.

La Tortilla Factory was named one of the "Best Places to Work" from the North Bay Business Journal six years in a row; in 2007, nearly 3,000 local employees and 117 larger companies participated. In 2011, they were also honored by the Small Business Administration as the top family business in the Western United States.

Lundberg Family Farms

The *Get-Along Factor* in Lundberg Family Farms is strong. Albert Lundberg, the patriarch, held God, land, and family close. When it came time to pass the farming, milling, and production to his sons, he divided it equally, yet didn't obligate them to farm for their life work. Albert and his four sons were known for early and frequent inclusion of young family members. Lundbergs are inclusive—methodically seeking everyone's input to reach a collective decision. Control is spread throughout the family, and respect of each other's intents and opinions is high; trust runs rampant.

Interiors Unlimited

The *Get-Along Factor* in Interiors Unlimited was low to non-existent. Neal had his older brother as a partner, but he bought him out after a few years in business together. Neal created interpersonal conflict between co-workers—family and non-family alike. When the current CEO, his son Tom, was about eleven, Neal got divorced from his first wife and within six months was married to Ruth, a close friend of the family.

Neal's marriage to Ruth brought her son, Don, into the business. The relationship between Tom and Don was strained from the beginning. Tom was used to working from an early age at summer jobs, supporting and putting himself through college. Don, on the other hand, had a sense of entitlement that was only trumped by his lack of ambition. While Tom was putting in sixty hour weeks, Don limped in with thirty to forty. Employees observed and questioned Don's dedication to the company, accusing him of pocketing money from side jobs on company time and with company materials. This was later confirmed. It followed the pattern of his stepfather, Neal, who would use the second company, N & R Supplies, to provide a smokescreen of tracking cash between the two companies, placing much of it into his personal bank account.

Relationships within the family and then within the business were guarded. The family communication pattern was predominately accusatory, blame finding, and attacking. Neal was verbally abusive, beginning in childhood and stretching into adulthood, telling vendors and employees that Tom is "hardheaded and stupid." This was not done privately, but in front of employees and other family members. Tom was also wrongly accused of not being adept at running the business while he was successfully managing large, profitable projects.

Forgiveness

Forgiveness is necessary for healthy family relationships. Small annoyances turn into grievances and resentments that build to anger. Ensuring that a small annoyance does not result in conflict requires frequent, open dialogue between family members, coupled with a change in the offending behavior.

Annoyance to Anger

Here's a small example of how annoyance can quickly turn to anger. I allowed a minor annoyance to turn into anger, simply because my sister does not send birthday cards. I would religiously mail birthday cards and presents to her, her husband, and daughter, yet I received nothing in return. I complained through my twenties and early thirties, my feelings moving from annoyance to resentment. When I was mature enough to step back and look at reality, I was able to acknowledge that I couldn't change her behavior. As my anger began to dissipate, I "forgave" her; she has so much to offer as a sister that to focus on this one small area would have robbed me of an important relationship.

Many of our expectations of others, what Dr. Luskin[7] coins "unenforceable rules," are ours to work through, not the other person's. When we continue to "rent space" in our thoughts to someone else's behavior, going over their actions, talking to others, building a bigger wall of resentment and anger, we are the ones who lose. We have allowed the other person to steal a big part of our life and peace.

Naming what behavior is in front of us and having a conversation with the "offender" can release the annoyance before it turns to anger. Some actions are merely annoyances that can be easily released, while other actions can lead straight to anger. A family member who frequently questions decisions might be seen as annoying, while one who purposefully underperforms or uses company equipment and funds for personal gain will trigger resentment and anger within the family and among employees.

Expectations & Reality

Forgiveness means that you stop wasting your time and energy being upset about another person's behavior, especially behavior that you have no control over. You practice forgiveness in order to care for yourself, not to condone bad behavior or stay in harm's way, but to free yourself and your inner thought life from the pain of holding grudges. When you have control over someone else's behavior—usually only with a power differential of parent-child or employer-employee—then you can set and expect certain behaviors. Even then, it is better to influence, build trust, and convince rather than demand.

Victim or Heroine

You are either the victim or heroine of your life. After childhood, you decide whether you allow others to negatively impact you or not; you can forgive them and move on or stay stuck in anger. The process of forgiveness includes talking about it, writing down expectations, and

---

7   *Forgive for Good: A Proven Prescription for Health and Happiness,* Frederic Luskin, 2003.

being realistic about the situation. It is a process where you move from victim to creator of your own destiny. It requires you to do frequent reality checks, learn how to let go, refocus, and create new experiences.

La Tortilla Factory

Carlos is good at having an on-going dialogue with his siblings. However, one of the areas that this may not have occurred with the breadth and depth needed was the determination of who would be the next CEO. Mike invested a lot of time and energy into the business, and there may have been an unspoken idea that, being the youngest, he would be the next in line to lead after Carlos. Carlos and Willie had an objective assessment done to determine who would become the next CEO, and the decision was made to recruit a non-family CEO.

While grudges are not commonly repeated and primary in their relationships, there have been some family grievances between some of the brothers who believed Carlos was too controlling about the way he handled the business. This led to estrangement of some family members from family events and holiday celebrations after a few brothers left the business. Other family members perceive the same events as Carlos being a visionary leader and building a sustainable business.

Lundberg Family Farms

Lundberg Family Farms' level of forgiveness between family members is high, most likely the highest of the three families because of the intense level of deliberative, frequent conversations that occur within the family and the company alike. It doesn't mean that they all fulfill each other's expectations, but there is an underlying acknowledgment that they generally "live and let live" as long as the basic family values are upheld. In this environment of acceptance, there is support and forgiveness. One of the younger generation members told me that "I don't go to church and I know of several others; it's simply assumed we do and no one says anything."

By the time a large decision is made, like the CEO direct report restructure or investment in a new administrative building, so much input and committee work has occurred that the chance of building resentments is unlikely.

Interiors Unlimited

Neal, at Interiors Unlimited, sought revenge, not forgiveness, in his relationships. His second wife, Ruth, supported his behavior against his son, pointing out all the possible weak points of Tom while shielding her son, Don. When the company entered into management succession, instead of gifting stock to his son, Tom, and stepson, Don, Neal proceeded to "give" them company stock in lieu of their bonus. A year later Neal demanded the stock be returned to him.

I was brought in to help them make this transition and when it became obvious that Neal was not going to let go and Ruth would not accept her son reporting to Tom, I bowed out. The revenge became so intense that Tom was forced to put a restraining order on his father to keep him physically away from company property.

Forgiveness and moving on were not a part of the Interiors Unlimited culture or the family culture; blame and finger-pointing ruled. Grievances became long-standing resentments that frequently resulted in outbursts of anger in front of employees.

Forgiving, Releasing & Moving On

Families in business have far greater interaction time, and therefore, more opportunities to disappoint each other. Learning to quickly and effectively air annoyances and resentments is an important part of building the healthy family foundation.

I visualize forgiveness as picking up pebbles in my life pathway, examining them, and deciding whether I can just toss them aside ("forgive and forget") or need to face the person and have a conversation. I have found that there are more annoyances in life that I can push aside than true breaks in trust and offensive behaviors. Forgiving others is hard;

forgiving a sibling can be like picking up and tossing a boulder instead of a pebble.

Sibling Rivalry

Sibling Roles: Driver, Eccentric, Entitled & Caretaker

I may be a driver early in the morning, writing reports, taking care of work tasks; by noon I may become the caretaker, helping a co-worker who is behind in their work; by 2 p.m. I may walk circles in the office, singing loudly off key, and by 3 p.m. I may feel entitled to take a nap. We each play different roles at different times, but we have a predominant style that best fits our personality, our family, and our workplace.

Roles are assumed in every family. Sometimes these roles are forced on children by their parents. Other times they are learned from observation or developed as a survival mechanism in an unhealthy family. Ideally, the role naturally unfolds from our personality, skills, and abilities. Some siblings are assertive, goal driven, independent, and want to contribute to the business; others want to explore different or more creative careers than what the business can offer; and still others feel entitled to take much and work little. The caretaker follows behind mending relationships, arranging events, and generally caring for the family.

Sibling Competition

As children, we compete for our parents' love and attention at the expense of our siblings by putting them down and building ourselves up. As we mature and develop, we release this need to appear superior. However, if our parents don't support our personal growth, we will bring our siblings fights into the business. This rivalry is seen in both subtle and open forms of competition for position, power, and control.

Parents deciding on the succession of the CEO position from one sibling to another should seek objective advisors to assist in the process. Emotional maturity, humility, and a good interpersonal relationship will help the sibling negotiate this leadership change. If the parents have already gifted most of their stock to their children, the struggle of a CEO change, absent an acting Board of Directors, lands in the lap of the siblings.

The Psychology Behind Sibling Rivalry

The relationship between brothers and sisters is fundamental to business success. We experience multiple societal stories about sibling rivalry ranging from verbal fighting to murder. The two sons of Adam and Eve were Cain, a crop farmer, and his younger brother Abel, the shepherd. Cain is portrayed as the greedy, jealous son who murders his brother, Abel. In Greek mythology, Ares versus Athena, Zeus versus Hera, and Proetus versus Acrisius are stories of sibling rivalry.

We, as parents, are usually drawn toward one sibling over another from a simple match of energy level, personality, and interests. For example, if a family values athletics and sports, a child who is a bookworm will be sidelined from a lot of activities and may feel devalued or isolated. Unfortunately, these feelings and relationships are not left in childhood. They are carried into adulthood and into the family business. The father who trusts the oldest son because they share similar interests and energy level may unknowingly shut down other siblings.

Sibling Bloodline Silos

Acting out behavior of siblings frequently mushrooms during a transition to the next generation. The temptation to "stay within bloodlines" leaves siblings running separate company divisions—a result of sibling rivalry gone wild. The reigning CEO will naturally be tempted to consider his sons or daughters for the CEO role. Developing a process to objectively consider all family and non-family CEO candidates will support business sustainability and family harmony.

Staying within the sibling family group is common in the second generation and potentially harmful. Ideally, siblings should report to aunts and uncles instead of their parents to discourage this silo effect. The focus on what business value, skills, and abilities each sibling brings should be the primary driver of decisions about who should report to whom. For example, if Corinne is good in finance, she should report to the CFO, her Uncle Jim, and not to her mother in operations.

La Tortilla Factory

La Tortilla Factory's second generation of independent Tamayo men set the stage for a sibling tug of war. Tico (Jose, Jr.), the second oldest, developed a strong career outside of the family business as a Wall Street financial executive. He did invest money in the family business, served as a Board member for many years, and was viewed as an important business advisor.

Bernie was very involved in the business at the beginning, managing the Mexi-catessen on weekends. His help was valuable in that it provided the family with at least one day off per week. Carlos tried to keep Bernie working in the business, but his calling was really in the social services. He resigned early on and returned to Omaha to work in a non-profit service organization.

Willie, from the beginning, was blessed with a gift for sales. He has the personality, intellect, and ability, and he soon became the major driver of sales that helped grow the company. Willie is skilled at telling the family story, selling the product quality, and building strategic alliances and relationships throughout the industry.

In the beginning, the youngest brother, Mike, was working in the company as the deli manager and as a route sales representative. Mike's calling was in production, reasearch and development, and quality. He utilized his unique gifts for creating new and innovative products. He developed La Tortilla's first low carb tortilla that Willie sold nationwide, subsequently making La Tortilla Factory a national company.

While there was some push and pull between Carlos and Willie around business practices, there was also an underlying base of respect between them that allowed the conversation to continue. Carlos talks openly about the fact that they were all raised to be driven, independent people and that may have gotten in the way of them getting along.

He specifically recalls that their mother was always telling them to "keep moving"; she and their father were role models of the benefit of perseverance and hard work.

Lundberg Family Farms

The Lundberg siblings began in the second generation with the four brothers. The brothers were used to working in the fields and milling operation together, learning from their father about the care of the land and family as all important. Whether it was the maturity of the parents or knowing that all hands were needed, Albert and Frances taught them to love, protect, and support each other. Stories are told of strong support and care between the brothers that seems to have translated down into the next two generations.

Interiors Unlimited

Tom knew that he and his siblings were at a disadvantage early on. Divorce and remarriage set the stage with brothers, sisters, stepbrothers, and stepsisters being drawn into conflict by the parents and stepparents. When Tom's dad Neal married Ruth (wife #2), she brought her two kids, Susan and Don, into the family. Don entered the business, but Susan did not.

Neal's two children, Tom and Kim, were in the business; Tom's involvement was steady and long-term, while Kim's was sporadic. Because Kim's relationship with her father was tortured, she left the business and distanced herself from Neal. The stepsibling rivalry was further weighted by them all being raised in different homes with different parents until they were in their early teens. It was a time when Tom distinctly remembers going from being an A student in school to barely passing, from loving to read to being unable to retain what he just read.

Neal's need to control and challenge pitted them all against each other. At one point he pushed so hard that Tom and his stepbrother joined forces against Neal—earnestly developing work agreements to prove to Neal that they could jointly lead the company. They both wanted Neal to transition out of the business operations, travel more with Ruth, and finally retire. As it became clear that Ruth was going to protect her son, Don, over Tom, and Don refused to actively engage in the business, he and Tom grew further apart. Tom continued to work long hours and grow the business while Don aligned with his mother and stepfather against Tom.

While it can be problematic, there is an upside to sibling rivalry. It is believed to be common and is often affectionately referred to as a normal part of growing up. If kept at a reasonable level, the jealousy, competition, and struggle can lead to positive results for the business.

However, this is not so for our next exploration together. Family secrets are frequently more painful and rarely, if ever, a positive for either the family or the business.

Questions for Chapter 2 – The Get-Along Factor:

1. How well do family members get along?

2. How would you describe the relationship you have with your siblings and cousins?

3. What are the communication patterns in your family?

4. Do you think the majority of family members want to continue supporting the family business?

5. How are resentments handled in the family?

"If you cannot get rid of the family skeleton, you may as well make it dance."

–GEORGE BERNARD SHAW

CHAPTER 3

FAMILY SECRETS

Secrets shake the foundation of the family and spill into the business. Hiding them is a joke. When I enter a business and interview a handful of family members, by the time I am done listening to the sixth person, I have heard the "hidden, untold" secrets from at least four of them.

Family secrets are the hidden underbelly that we do not want others to see. Generally it is the behavior of one or a few in the family that we hide, control, excuse, and try to fix. Uncle Jim is always happier in the afternoon at work... well, yes, he had a few drinks at lunch, but he's harmless.

The more transparent we are about family secrets, the more supportive we can be of each other. A pattern of directly addressing family problems will carry over into the culture of the business.

Substance Abuse

The most common family secret is alcoholism and drug abuse. Illegal drug use and alcoholism impacts the full family and is frequently multi-generational in its reach. Many different circumstances can lead to substance abuse: genetic predisposition, mental illness, chronic physical pain, chaotic family life, societal influence, or lack of self-esteem, just to name a few.

Most families hide and minimize the problem until the legal system is involved. The initial use of drugs and alcohol by a person in their teens and early twenties in these families is often a cry for help, a way to numb the pain that they have felt living in their disconnected family.

When the alcoholic is the CEO and the father of the family, the damage to the children puts the next generation and business sustainability at risk. I've worked with many family businesses where the father is a functional alcoholic. In other words, he's a hard driving workaholic who is able to build a substantial business, but evenings at home are dominated by shouting matches that sometimes end in physical violence.

The other route is the alcoholic who mellows after a few drinks and passes out. Both are unavailable to their families. Children will either withdraw or act out, unless the abuser and family get well. The child that internalizes the family pain may become depressed or even suicidal. They will often harm themselves by drinking, using, cutting, and overachieving. Eating disorders, anorexia and bulimia, are also common among teenage girls when one or both parents is emotionally unavailable.

Recovery from alcoholism or substance abuse almost always requires professional help for the extended family as well as the identified user. Involving a combination of residential and outpatient treatment will increase the chance of success. The involved professionals and community support groups should have in-depth experience with addiction recovery.

Behavior Extreme

Sexual abuse within the family is frequently connected with substance abuse. Emotionally unavailable alcoholic parents create role confusion, with older siblings taking on a parental role and sometimes sexually abusing younger siblings. A parent who sexually abuses a son or daughter triggers deep emotional pain that may take years, if not decades, to unearth and heal.

Behaviors of excess—spending, gambling, overworking, drinking, and raging—are thrill seeking addictions that mask an emotional emptiness in the person's life. They may also be the result of substance abuse or a chemical imbalance. These behaviors are supported by easy access to money, attorneys, and cushy rehab programs.

Finances

Finances? Really?! Yes, this is frequently a family secret. And the number one stated cause for divorce is disagreement on money management. In the family business, how money is valued, spent, saved, and invested is often hidden. Did Grandpa hold on to every last penny? Did he work harder on evading Uncle Sam than developing new revenue streams? Was there family agreement on how to reinvest into the business and what to save in reserve, or was this the sole decision of the founder? Are family members and employees paid a fair salary?

Financial overindulgence of a generation is at the other end of the spectrum. Parent guilt starts this pattern of excessive giving to children. Let's face it, business start-ups can be exciting, stressful, and time intensive. Dad is gone a lot, feels guilty, and tries to balance the lack of time by giving credit cards, cars, resort vacations, and other things. Some adult children continue the pattern by taking from the business—entitlement sets in.

Many business owners assist key employees, family and non-family, with personal loans, housing, and education in a haphazard way that hurts both the business and the person being helped. This giving blurs the boundaries between business and personal.

Trading and Giving Away Products and Services

If you let me use your forklift this weekend, I'll give you two cases of our wine. Trading the services of the family business for use of a friend's equipment is common, as is donating product to a child's school raffle, swapping services for services, etc. Yes, we want to do this because it skirts the formality of purchasing each other's products and services, builds friendships, and avoids Uncle Sam. That may all be true; however, it is frequently not an even trade, kills friendships, decreases employee morale, and creates a "who is getting more" pile of resentments within the family.

This is a very tempting area. I admit that I have personally traded and so has my husband. I also assert that we no longer do it.

This is not just the arena of the small family business. I watched as two CEOs from large companies swapped inventory for personal use. One of the gentlemen was happy with his trade; the other brought down a family Christmas celebration when it was discovered.

Swapping and trading frequently is not seen as taking company assets, but it is a slippery slope that is truly a misuse of company resources.

Embezzlement

Family members embezzle. There I said it. It shocks us. And as tough and painful as this one is, it is not as uncommon as many of us would like to think. It lands under family secrets because we rarely involve the police and district attorney the way we do if it's a non-family member.

How could this happen? There are many factors leading to this: chronic financial strain, a general sense of family entitlement, lack of internal company controls, the reality or perception of being overworked and underpaid. I am not excusing the behavior; I'm simply saying I understand the circumstances that can lead to personal justification.

Here's an example of how it can start small and quickly grow: I fill up my gas tank once on a Friday and pay for it with the business account, knowing that it will be primarily for personal, not business use. I tell myself it's okay because I have filled the tank on my own some weekends and used "my gas" for business on Monday and Tuesday. Then I take a few vacation days and don't record it as paid time off. I pick up gift cards for employee recognition and pocket a few for myself. I know that Dad pays me less than local competitors, and this is the way I even it out. I notice other family members treating the business the same way, so it simply becomes the "way we do things around here"—it is our company culture, not embezzlement.

The misuse of company assets, time, and money escalates. A non-working family member is added to payroll, petty cash disappears, one out of ten customer checks are rerouted to a personal account, and personal items are consistently charged to the business credit card. Eventually, an employee in accounting notices and agonizes about who and when to tell.

Action is required; a cautious, thoughtful, respectful approach is wise. A pre-meeting, without the suspect family member, will address the following:

1. Do we have clear, hard, verifiable facts before we assume fault and intent?

2. Who will be at the meeting to lay the facts out?

3. Are we going to involve the legal system?

4. If we continue employment with this family member, do we need to change their job position?

5. How or will we message this to the rest of the family? To other employees? To the Board of Directors?

6. How or did the company contribute to this problem?

7. If the company did, what steps will we take to prevent it in the future?

8. How or did the family contribute to this problem?

9. If the family did, what steps will we take, as a family, to prevent it in the future?

10. Has this family member had chronic, known problems with finances?

11. Generally, how can we protect the company from future misuse of company assets or embezzlement?

12. How do we protect the whistleblower?

13. Do we have a whistleblower program set-up internally? Are employees trained annually?

14. Do we talk openly in Family Council about our responsibility to financially protect and care for company assets? Do we give specific examples of what is and is not allowed?

15. Do we have a solid non-compete clause in our employment contracts and/or employee handbook in case we have to release the family member from employment?

16. Do we consistently run a professional background check on applicants?

17. If I need to walk them out the door, how do I prepare? Computer security, locks, passwords, current company asset retrieval, bank account access protection, social media tracking, last paycheck, etc.

18. Do we need to involve the corporate attorney, Board of Directors, outside legal attorney, CPA, business psychologist? If so, when and how?

The second meeting (with the suspect family member) should stay at the level of discovery—laying out facts and asking the family member their perception of what happened. This is assuming that the embezzlement is not excessive. We need to be vigilant in checking ourselves, asking "What would I do if this wasn't a family member?" and "Is this at a level where I will be able to trust them again?"

Family Anxiety and Sibling Isolation

A disturbing sibling situation is the singling out of one child as the target of poor treatment, ranging from minor teasing to physical abuse. This abuse may involve one or both parents, as well as siblings. One of my clients described it as, "I knew I was bad because I wasn't included and was always picked on—deep down I knew something was wrong with me; I just didn't know what it was." This child holds the family's anxiety, unresolved emotional issues, and pain.[8]

The isolated child goes through three stages of ostracism: 1) being ignored, excluded, or verbally or physically abused, 2) coping, and 3) resignation. Being excluded will lead to a coping mechanism of either shutting down or acting out. This communication and interaction

---

8   Dr. Murray Bowen & Michael E. Kerr; *Family Education*, 1988.

pattern will follow the family into the business. The identified "bad child" fulfills the family's vision by being a low performer. As the abused sibling matures, they may choose to leave the family business if the bad treatment continues. If this adult child begins to understand the family role they are playing, and refuses to allow it to continue, the family will either acknowledge their part in this dance or not. If family members own up to the pattern, healing can begin. If the family doesn't heal, they will seek out a new target to place their anxiety on, frequently a non-family employee in a leadership position.

Jim[9], a non-family employee, climbed from his original position as a building inspector to a licensed architectural engineer in a family business. He "became like one of the family" with his employment longevity, inclusion in family events, and acknowledged contribution to the growth and success of the company. When the underperforming son, Calvin, left the business and moved across the country, the family seemed to be at a loss. Jim talked about being surprised that the family was so concerned about the move because they complained constantly about Calvin's work. Jim explains what he viewed as a strange occurrence:

> *"I expected a sense of relief to occur, but what I noticed was outbursts of anger and random verbal sniping of employees. I was in transition, before Calvin's move, to become the CEO with Dave, one of their other sons, holding the COO position. I assumed the CEO role, but where I had been golden, I now was taking daily complaints about my leadership style, decisions, and results. Things would calm down for a few weeks and then erupt directly at me. Instead of problem solving a project misstep or client complaint, they would personally blame me for everything that went wrong. After a few years, and some professional help, I came to understand that I had assumed Calvin's role in the family and I quietly bowed out. I have been in a new firm for three years now and am still baffled by what I experienced."*

---

9   Based on actual client, but not one of the three case studies we are following; industry and names changed.

Obviously, this level of dysfunction can cause great harm to the individual, family, and business. Be alert for the "family black sheep or trouble maker," watching to see if it is truly that individual or if it is part of the family dynamic. This is a time for professional intervention. Grab a licensed Marriage Family Therapist to work through this situation.

Chronic Physical and Mental Illness

Chronic mental and physical illness of one family member will increase the stress level of the core and extended family unit. An early diagnosis, professional help, and periodic relief for the family caretaker are essential to keep the family intact. The extent of the challenge will determine if and how much it will impact the business.

When Families Fall Apart

If there are multiple levels of family secrets—substance use, gambling, anger and divorce—it is easy to understand the challenge it places on the business. It may be possible to manage during the first generation, but during the subsequent generations, it will be difficult to transition if there is a pile of unresolved pain and drama. Family businesses that are in their fourth and fifth generation are healthy families, not perfect, but stable, thoughtful, and functional. They encourage individual growth and development, support their nieces and nephews, and don't resort to alcohol or drugs to deaden pain. Rather, they speak openly about what hurts and what doesn't work.

A spiritual focus or religious practice can add to family cohesiveness or stability. Of course, this is not always so. One client example pops into my mind of a "practicing" Catholic family who fought constantly, treated their employees poorly, and had family members struggling with alcoholism, anorexia, and anger. However, for many families, a faith community and practice of religious tenets can be positive forces.

Questions for Chapter 3 – Family Secrets:

1. How do we handle family secrets, such as addictions or other destructive behavior?

2. How have we handled chronic physical and/or mental illness within our family?

3. Is trading company products and services a common practice in our business? What has and hasn't worked with this practice?

4. What are our company's procedures, policies, controls and training around the proper handling of business finances?

5. How have we handled a divorce or separation in our family? Are we prepared for both the emotional and financial implications?

We have explored the many complexities of families and its interaction with the business. Let's now turn our focus to the talent within the business.

"The person born with a talent they are meant to use will find their greatest happiness in using it."
–JOHANN WOLFGANG VAN GOETHE

CHAPTER 4

MOVING TALENT AROUND THE TABLE:
EMPLOYEES, LEADERS & SUCCESSION

Understanding Business Talent Needs

A critical function for any business is attracting and retaining talent. Finding a person with the right mix of skills, attitude, drive, character, and experience that matches your business can be overwhelming; sometimes it just boils down to whether they show up on a daily basis. Okay, that might be a little extreme, but you've likely had a few missteps with the heavenly interview and perfect hire who turns into a nightmare exactly three months later.

Identifying talent requires you to look critically at the functions that support business growth and to create job descriptions that describe the level of experience, education, and skills you need when hiring. Implementing a fair compensation system, employee recognition program, performance evaluation system, and career path are all a part of retention. Helping people develop and stretch their abilities will keep them challenged and engaged.

Matching Family Talent to Business Need

Matching the family talent to the business need should follow your overall plan for talent management. Unfortunately, many family businesses do it in the opposite order, placing the family member where they want to be versus deciding where, or if, they will bring value to the company. Hiring in this manner may not only cause you to bypass great external talent, but it can also create frustration and resentment among current employees who will be forced to work with a family member who is ill prepared for the job.

A healthy company will only fill open positions using a competitive process with multiple applicants. Everything being equal, it is assumed that the family member will get the final advantage, but only after a fair and thoughtful process. Employee morale is quickly destroyed when hiring and retention practices clearly favor family members. This also includes internal promotions. One astute family member in her late twenties told me, "I can't just be good. Being the daughter of the CEO, I feel a great pressure to exceed [expectations] and set an example of how the family cares... how we are hard workers, not slackers."

The second common misstep is hiring at the incorrect level; a family member straight out of an MBA program, without work history, will sometimes assume they will start at a Director or Vice President level. Bringing the family member in over other employees who have managed for years and worked their way up the career ladder is a recipe for disaster. On the other extreme, I have seen family businesses that insist that every entering family member must "sweep the shop floor" or "visit customers in the field." If an adult child has finished their college education and has worked at a competitors for three to five years, asking them to quit being a controller for six months to sweep floors may push them to decline the "opportunity" to work at the family business. If they don't like sweeping floors more than they like playing with spreadsheets, but do it anyway, resentment is bound to be carried into business and family interactions. To top it all off, this practice discourages family talent from maximizing their contribution to company growth. If this "pay your dues" period is not required of other entering employees, why would you force it on your family? Well, there could be reasons, but we're not talking about the joy of retaliation right now!

Preparing Family Talent

Preparing family talent is the next step in ensuring that the business reaches the next generation. The Family Council can help the next generation by having a separate session for children between the ages of eight to eighteen to learn about the business. Understanding the skills, education, and experience they will need to enter the family business will give them time to think and prepare.

Some family businesses assist in preparing family members by fully or partially subsidizing their higher education costs. Depending on the business, that may be a technical institute certificate or an advanced college degree. One client I worked with generously educated their third generation by paying for fifty percent of their education during college and then reimbursing the other fifty percent after three successful years of employment in the family business. While the general population weighs in at thirty percent of people wielding college degrees[10], this family has ninety percent.

Positions & Requirements

A clear understanding of the skills and abilities your company needs, now and in the future, is essential for sustainability. A documented organizational reporting structure, along with written job descriptions, will begin the process. Creating a culture where employees understand their impact and see a future for themselves is just as important as defining a financial goal.

Family Integration Process

"The worst form of inequality is to try to make unequal things equal."

–ARISTOTLE

Transparent Entry

Will your children be line staff, managers, or leaders? All children do not develop equally, nor do they have similar goals and aspirations. Some of the most heart-wrenching family discussions center on the requirements for employment in the business. Allowing errant, irresponsible adult

---

10   *Educational Attainment in the United States: 2011;* U.S. Census Bureau, retrieved February 2012

children to enter is disruptive at best and usually destructive. Employees resent doing that person's job on top of their own, and other family members see it as a gold embossed invitation for their own carefree entry. Family members begin to believe that they have a right to employment regardless of their skills or performance.

Integrating family members into the business should begin as early as possible, with children being aware of the skills needed in the business and working age adults aware of what is required for entry. Each family member should know that they will be treated like every other employee.

Typically, other staff members expect family members to care more and work harder. Therefore, each family member needs to build on the business culture (in a positive way) through their actions. If the family shows a solid work ethic, it will be noticed and copied. On the other hand, if they practice poor work habits and use the business as their own personal checkbook, it will also be noticed, and either resented or adopted.

Expectations

Proactively setting employment expectations is crucial. Does the family member need to apply through the company's Human Resources department? Are they introduced into the business via the Family Council? Is an individualized job description okay to develop? Can they enter without an open position? Can they make a business case for a new position?

Family businesses vary in their approach. Some must go through Human Resources for a current open position, work outside of the family business for three years, and then build a business model to demonstrate the value they will bring. These agreements are frequently written in a Family Employment Guideline that is created by the Family Council.

Line of Report

Do you report to your uncle, cousin, or perhaps even your wife? Yes, we all know that at home we all report to Mom. But at work, reporting to a close family member is tough. When the company is small, it is sometimes unavoidable. Just as managers are warned against developing friendships with the people they supervise, having one family member supervising another is a recipe for conflict. If it must be, then it is better for a nephew to report to his uncle than a son to report to his father. A niece reporting to her aunt versus her mother also assists in a healthy mixture between bloodlines while making it easier to hold performance expectations.

Non-Family Employee Integration Process

Non-Family Employee Support

Non-family members, especially when they are new to the company, need to feel included and valued for their contributions. Too often, family business founders who have experienced stretches of minimal to no pay, expect non-family members to work below a normal wage. It feels silly to have to say it, but you need to pay competitively, for both family and non-family.

Employees commonly complain that they are placed in the middle of family dynamics—from delivering messages between brothers who aren't talking to blatant yelling in front of employees. Far from being supportive of the non-family employee, this asks them to do some extra heavy lifting to survive. As much as possible, separating family from business will help employees feel more engaged. In fact, something as simple as calling your father "John" instead of "Dad" will go a long way in professionalizing the workplace and leveling the playing field for everyone.

General Employee Integration

The family history, values, and commitment to the business can create a sense of shared ownership and care that is difficult to replicate in the non-family business. This can start during the application process and definitely during orientation. Carlos frequently refers to employees as extended family and talks about the number of other non-Tamayo, multi-generation families within the business.

When employees observe the owners practicing company values, they are more likely to adopt the same behaviors. It will show you who is or isn't a fit and allow you to refine your values.

Embracing the Non-Family Leader

When a family business member utters the words, "Let's consider a non-family CEO," the first reply is usually a colorful, "NO!" The reasons tumble out: *"They won't care as much," "They can't be as loyal as family," "The community and industry will wonder what is happening," "This CEO won't know how to manage the family."* In fact, non-family CEOs can be a great strategy for business sustainability and family harmony.

A non-family CEO frequently brings diverse, in-depth experience to drive business growth, bringing professional alliances, partnerships, and strategy opportunities. They can be a great mentor for the next generation of family leaders—often then known as a "bridge CEO" from one generation to the next. While the family may hold all the stock, it is critical to develop a performance incentive that will reward and retain the non-family CEO and an employment agreement that will fairly treat and protect the CEO.

Some family businesses address the desire to maintain stock ownership by developing phantom stock plans based on performance incentives for the non-family CEO and other key managers. This protects from actually distributing company stock, which is valued periodically, while the phantom stock reflects the shareholder value created during their employment.

What is it like being an executive leader as a non-family member? While there is an added layer of complexity managing the business and the family, success can bring a deep sense of satisfaction and achievement. And, just like using exercise and good eating to minimize a middle age spread, there are strategies and governance structures to support healthy family interactions with a non-family CEO.

Succession

Letting Go

CEO longevity in non-family businesses is an average of six years, versus family owned businesses whose CEOs tend to stay for 20-25 years. What attributes to this gap? Often, one sibling is chosen after the death of the ruling matriarch or patriarch, and that person remains until their retirement. Some noted positives are leadership stability and consistency. The negatives can include flat growth, narrow business focus, and decreasing leadership drive.

When the CEO and other top level executive family members do not step aside in an orderly and timely fashion, it causes a high level of frustration in the next generation that's ready for a shot at leadership. This is a touchy period when many midsize family businesses lose talented adult children who are ready to charge forward, while parents, aunts, and uncles are unwilling or unprepared to leave. Once it becomes clear that the children might reach their mid to late fifties before taking over, it becomes hard to hold on to the ambitious ones.

Letting go is complicated by poor financial planning. The leader may have been personally financing many of the ups and downs of the business, leaving their wealth tied to it. Early and frequent planning with a team of advisors (certified financial planner, estate planning lawyer, certified public accountant, and corporate lawyer) is essential for the owner to be able to step back and allow the next generation to lead.

Letting go is scary. It brings up issues of mortality. Once, a leader told me: "Admitting to retirement is the same as saying I have one foot in the grave and the other will soon follow." How many times have you heard that "he will never leave his job, but will be carried out feet first"? The fear of death can reach a clinical level. Symptoms include feelings of uncontrollable anxiety, obsessive thoughts about death, a persistent and overwhelming fear, desire to flee, a feeling of powerlessness, and possibly full blown panic attacks.

The sense of powerlessness is strong when letting go of the known for the unknown. That's why preparing for retirement by building financial stability, outside hobbies, and friendships will help keep one's fear of death from escalating.

Leaders often build their business from the ground up, pouring in their time, money, and effort at the steep expense of family relationships. Those who escape without divorce or uncontrollable teenagers find that resentments have built a wall around their loved ones. The business is often seen as "my baby and life," making it difficult to turn the care over to a successor.

Letting go of the business can feel like a clear admission of your mortality. Depending on your values and level of self-reflection, this step can be a minor or serious challenge. One CEO put it well, in that even with external friendships, a supportive wife, wanting to travel, and a consuming hobby of restoring antique cars, he felt highly anxious and sometimes deeply depressed when he thought of turning the company over to his capable daughter. One day when he was out fishing his mortality hit him. He noticed younger men easily traversing up and down the sides of the very steep lakeshore, and then he saw an older gentleman leaning against his son to walk down to the water's edge and gently lower himself into a chair. He knew then that leaving his CEO role signaled to him that he was nearing the end of his life. "I broke out in a sweat watching that father and son, thinking all the while of my daughter taking over the company."

Some CEOs begin to relinquish their role by taking up the role of President or Chairman of the Board. They may view the role of President as the outside family "face" of the company, helping with alliances and partnerships that could further expand the reach and profitability of the company. Other CEOs focus on transitioning to the role as Chairman of the Board, possibly bringing on the first non-family board members and establishing good governance practices.

Leader Selection

Who's next? Many family businesses make this choice based on seniority (i.e. — "She's the oldest, so she will be our next CEO."). In some families, the next in line is the oldest male. Moving to a more professional process of skill evaluations, performance assessments, and reviews of career history seems foreign to many families' decision processes. A single owner can make the easy decision to pass the business leadership to the child of their choice. But this "easy" choice can backfire if the adult child has not gained respect from other family members and employees. And even if there are good relationships, not including the family in a conversation about a leadership change can lead to conflict and alienation.

The more thoughtful, objective, and inclusive the process of bringing on the next leader, the more likely that the transition will be embraced. Succession readiness calls for a written transition plan and an individual development plan for the future CEO within three years of the planned succession date. Implementation of the plan may involve identifying other executive team members with succession needs, building a coaching plan, and providing stretch assignments in different functional areas of the company.

While succession planning can happen at any level within the organization, we commonly think about the top five to eight key positions for a written, structured succession plan. The position that gets the most attention for succession planning is CEO. One of the noted pitfalls to consider is lack of advanced planning and agreement on an acceptable retirement date.

La Tortilla Factory

La Tortilla Factory places value and emphasis on education. They expect many of their front-line managers and leaders to have advanced degrees and encourage that by offering flex schedules so they can complete their college educations. They also have a partial scholarship program for employees who are furthering their education in areas that will bring value to the business. For example, they will assist in food science and business degrees. This education extends to line staff in areas such as time management, communication skills, and English as a Second Language.

Jonna Greene, Vice President of Operations, began in La Tortilla Factory as the Human Resource Director and worked her way up to the executive leadership team. During her tenure in human resources, she understood the value the family placed on education, and with Carlos' agreement, instituted employee education and training programs throughout the organization. Working well within the family business, she balanced finding the best talent and integrating family members into the business.

Carlos, Willie, and Mike were the primary executive team for many years, with Carlos leading operations, Willie leading sales and marketing, and Mike leading production and Research & Development. As the company grew and expanded, they were strategic and deliberative about bringing in other high-level professionals versus continuing to place family members in those areas. They hired several external sales and marketing professionals who built their careers in much larger companies. They committed, early on, to healthy products, and subsequently added a research and development function staffed with highly educated personnel, both family and non-family.

In 2006, when Carlos turned 60 he began thinking about stepping down from his CEO role; he brought in a trusted family business consulting firm to interview the executive management team, talk to family members, and conduct a professional   assessment of potential leaders. Carlos also had an organizational assessment completed that looked at the business culture and overall talent management of the company. Carlos thoughtfully considered employee input, family input, and the consulting firms' findings to arrive at the next leader—Stan Mead, a non-family member who was currently serving as the Chief Financial Officer. It sounds simple, but it required many heart-wrenching decisions, including not placing his son or his youngest brother in the position.

Both Carlos transitioning out of the CEO position and Willie out of the Executive VP of Sales position were intentional in letting go and allowing others to step into those roles and make them their own. Carlos refocused his attention to becoming the Chairman of the Board of Directors, bringing in their first outside members, while Willie continued in a role of supporting the Vice President of Sales and maintaining the positive Tamayo family presence in the market. Willie also became very active working with several non-profit youth organizations in the local community.

Lundberg Family Farms

The Lundbergs have followed a steady march of leadership through family agreement and seniority. Albert (the company's original leader), passed on his leadership to his four sons, Eldon, Wendell, Harlan, and Homer, as if they were one, and they informally had Eldon, the oldest, lead. While Eldon led, it was rare for him to assert himself. The family style was to gather information and opinions, and to talk until a decision was reached. The four brothers had an ongoing dialogue and agreement on business decisions, meeting twice a week to review rice production and product development. Frequently the four would hop into a truck to go look at their rice fields.

As the company grew and became more complex, they formed a Board of Directors with Eldon, the eldest, as Chair. When Eldon was nearing 70, he announced his retirement would be in the next few months and that the leadership would be handed over to the next eldest brother, Wendell. Eldon was seen by the next generation as providing a vote of confidence in their ability to lead the company forward. Shortly after the Board of four brothers assembled, they added a child from each of the four brothers to represent their bloodline on the Board. Jessica, Wendell's daughter, remembers being just out of college, in her early 20s, trying to figure out where she fit in the company and at the same time, serving as a member of the Board of Directors.

Approximately two years after Wendell assumed leadership, he handed the role to Harlan, who then handed it to Homer a year later. The brothers quickly and in an orderly manner passed leadership to the third generation. Jessica, Wendell's daughter, was elected by the Board of Directors as the Chair in 2005.

At Lundberg, several family members and senior team members mentioned that while the company pays competitively, both in compensation and benefits, Grant, the family CEO, doesn't draw as much as he deserves.

The Lundbergs are adopting a policy for family members entering employment. Their policy is to create a position for family members if one does not exist. Homer (the fourth of the four brothers) noted that his oldest brother, Eldon, believed that if real potential and ability was shown by a family member, you should bring them in, regardless of an open position, because that person will "make an area of your business profitable."

Lundberg Family Farms have a history of including non-family employees. The four brothers shared equally from the beginning, taking the same salary and returns. As the company expanded, they've moved from the share alike philosophy, to bonuses based on how someone, family or non-family, is contributing to the growth. The farm portion also has a profit sharing plan, as well as healthcare and benefits for the laborers.

One of the talent challenges that Lundberg faces is one that all growth companies face—integration of loyal, long-term employees with the infusion of new talent. This challenge requires diligence and commitment to both bringing long-term employees forward with training and learning a new skill, to assessing performance and reviewing expectations. It is also finding the balance between holding onto low performers because "we're a family business" versus recognition that the shareholders (family) deserve a fair return on their capital investment, and that other family and non-family management deserve compensation for a job well done.

Interiors Unlimited

While Neal allowed family members into the business, there was no forethought of how to integrate them and best use their talents. Once they were on board, Neal asked them to work long hours with minimal pay. Of course, he didn't limit this to just family members. Tom jokingly noted that his dad had two requirements for employees—first, they needed to have a DUI (driving under the influence) conviction, and second, they would have to agree to be paid for 32 hours while working 50 or 60. The thought behind this was that they would have a hard time being employed for their conviction of drunk driving and would therefore be obligated to him, effectively binding them to him.

The philosophy was much like that in the early industrial period in America, where large lumber mills and coal mines would own the housing that was rented to their workers, and would give their employees/tenants credit at the company's general store. Between paying for housing and food, people working in lumber mills and coal mines would often become obligated to the owner. In the same way, Neal sought unemployable people, paid low rates, and further obligated many of them by making personal advance loans to help them out with housing and transportation.

Throughout his tenure, Neal had many family members working for him, including his wife, second wife, son, stepson, daughter, nephew, and daughter-in-law. Neal was consistently critical of family talent, except for himself and his second wife. Neal was known to fire and reinstate family employment in the span of four hours for small mistakes.

Neal had no desire to transition his business to his children. He did successfully plan for his retirement and had the money to do it, but he actively blocked his son and stepson from moving forward. His business had become his life and he enjoyed the control of it and of family members. Neal's second wife, Ruth, pressed Neal to travel, but when he had days off away from the business, he would become very depressed, sitting in his chair at home and watching TV all day. Although he and Ruth were taking longer and longer trips during the last five years, whenever he was home he wanted to be in the office.

When the plan was established to transition some of his activities to his stepson Don and other office staff, he would release some of the information but retain a good portion of it. Then he'd watch carefully to catch Don failing. One of the on-going challenges for Tom and Don was that Neal would go around them to discipline and direct employees.

Eventually, they all began spending time trying to catch each other doing things wrong. For example, they started tracking each other's miles, trying to discover who put gas into cars and recreational vehicles for personal use. They were also spending their weekends re-examining invoices and payments to catch each other doing something incorrect. Tom felt compelled to check job orders, as he had indications that Don was doing side jobs with company product and time, while putting the profit into his pocket. Soon, lawsuits started flying back and forth, primarily targeted from Neal to Tom, and the court appointed a receiver to take over management of the company. The receiver and his staff investigated and determined that Don was detrimental to the company and released him from employment.

Neal continued to sue his biological son, Tom, for various causes. He would change the selling price of the business, pull back stock ownership, and try to interfere with the daily operations to the point that Tom was required to hire his own legal counsel and place a restraining order on Neal. As Tom put it, Neal's sole purpose in life became thinking about how he could hurt Tom and destroy the business that he created rather than see it pass to his son.

This has been extremely painful for the family and has resulted in a long-term, if not permanent, separation, between father and son.

Fortunately, Tom watches for and encourages family talent. Even after the split between himself and his father, he employs family members that are from other branches of the family. Tom carefully assesses people. For example, his nephew Phillip was working out in the field, suffered a minor injury, and was placed in the office during his recovery. Tom noted that Phillip did very well at scheduling and organizing in estimating, so he kept him in the office and replaced Phillip's field position with a new hire. Likewise, Tom knew his daughter had great business acumen. After she worked her way up in another company, he brought her into the company as his right-hand operations person.

Questions for Chapter 4 – Moving Talent Around the Table: Employees, Leaders, & Succession:

1. How does your business identify talent needs?

2. How do family members find out about open positions?

3. How do the children of the family begin to learn about the business?

4. Describe the level of support for educating family members.

5. Do family members go through the company's Human Resource department to apply for an open position?

6. What are leaders doing to prepare for their retirement from the business?

7. If you are the CEO, what is your fear level of letting go of the leadership position?

8. Is there clarity about the succession of senior level positions? Who will be next? When? How do they need to develop further?

"Leadership and learning are indispensable to each other."
–JOHN F. KENNEDY

CHAPTER 5

WHO'S AT THE
HEAD OF THE TABLE:
FAMILY BUSINESS GOVERNANCE

Governance

Who is providing financial oversight of the company? Evaluating the leader? Guiding the succession of the next leaders? Approving strategic direction? Who is overseeing estate planning and ownership transfer?

Whether you use a Board of Directors, Advisory Committee, or family around the kitchen table approach, governance of the family business is crucial to successful transition of the business to the next generation. The Board of Directors is the highest governing body of the company after your Annual Shareholders' Meeting. Early individual financial planning, coupled with estate planning and business ownership transfer planning, will serve the family well in transitioning into the next generation. The governance structures—Annual Shareholder Meeting, Board of Directors, and Family Council—support these planning efforts.

Membership

Most family boards have membership according to the bloodlines of the family. In other words, if the original owner has five children, you will commonly see six seats on the board—one representative from each adult child's family and the owner parent. One family member will serve on the Board of Directors and the Family Council, providing linkage and coordination between these two governing bodies. While we have already admitted that younger family organizations may have someone playing the role of manager and board member, this is strongly discouraged. The Chief Executive Officer is typically the only company employee that occupies a seat on the board; the Chief Financial Officer or Chief Operating Officer may present occasionally at board meetings, but should not be in regular attendance.

As the business matures, adding outside, non-family expertise to the board is important. The needed proficiency of these people may include an extensive financial background, such as a retired CFO, an industry expert, an innovator, or another high level executive from another company. The board members should be carefully selected, not generally friends of the family, and not existing professional advisors to the business. An optimal size is between five to nine members.

Rules and Responsibilities

There is a juggling of hats and roles with family boards. You may be the majority shareholder, Chairman of the Board, and Chief Executive Officer (CEO) in the company, as well as husband and father...yikes! Knowing when to put on your shareholder, CEO, or father hat is a delicate skill. Something as silly as announcing, "I am now speaking as the CEO, not your father," can be a good way to signal the change in conversation and authority level.

There are family boards that also have a board member who is working further down in the organizational structure, such as a first line manager that is now privy to company strategic direction conversations and decisions they would normally not be involved in. This family manager must practice diplomacy with peers, restraining from throwing out the "I sit on the Board of Directors" card when they want their way in some workplace decision. Learning to influence within their current role limitation as manager is challenging when they have the real or perceived power of board membership tucked away in their back pocket.

The role of the Board of Directors is to:

1. Review and approve business strategy.

2. Review financial performance and hold top leadership accountable for that performance.

3. Select, evaluate, and compensate the Chief Executive Officer.

4. Work with and advise the CEO.

5. Oversee the succession and continuity planning of the business (Chief Executive Officer and other key leadership positions).

6. Protect the interest of the shareholders.

7. Bring a fresh, outside perspective and ask insightful questions.

8. Ensure ethical conduct of management and the corporation.

9. Review risk management practices of the company.

10. Track estate planning and ownership transfer.

11. Review of their own board performance.

The board provides strategic direction, reviewing the vision and mission for relevancy and setting financial growth goals. Some boards actively create the strategic plan, but most leave that level of work to the CEO and her leadership team; the strategic plan is brought to the board for review and approval. Board members can refocus leadership from internal issues to an external strategic market and customer perspective.

The board has fiscal oversight on its plate of duties—approving the annual operational budget, requesting and reviewing audit reports, reviewing and questioning quarterly financial statements, and approving capital budgets. Board members should be knowledgeable about bank relationships, debt, and the status of bank covenants. The board's oversight of the annual financial audit includes follow-up on management notes from the auditors. Board members should be skilled in reading, understanding and questioning financial statements and controls.

CEO evaluation is next on the board's to-do list. A period of evaluation allows space for reflecting on the strengths, weaknesses, and development of the CEO. It also is a time for the board to reflect on how they could better support both the CEO and their own functioning as a board. While compensation structures may focus on the singular measure of company financial performances, the CEO's leadership style, innovation, vision, and ability to retain and influence talent should be part of the written evaluation. The board should also weigh in on the CEO's ability to keep the family engaged in understanding the business.

The board ensures the CEO's compensation package is structured to incentivize his retention and performance. Generally a formula, based on company financial performance, is layered on top of the base. An annual look at the compensation package, along with an objective outside review every third year, will bring another best practice to your company.

Family CEOs are frequently underpaid. While the family CEO might agree to this underpayment, the board needs to be concerned about the replacement cost of the CEO in the event of a sudden disability or death, and they need to consider the other ripple effects of not offering the CEO competitive payment for his or her leadership. This is an area riddled with feelings and value—self-worth, rivalry, jealousy, loyalty, fairness—therefore, it's an emotional stew that needs time to process before objectivity can enter.

One of the reasons it is important for any family member, but particularly high level management, to work outside the family business is the sense of accomplishment and confidence that is gained. A CEO who has proven their worth in one or several other companies will bring expertise, experience, and skills to the family company. This will increase their worth in their own eyes and from the perspective of board members and family shareholders. It is hard for "little Jimmy", who was the kid hanging out with Dad at work, to transform into a respected CEO without outside experience.

The board is also responsible, in closely held enterprises, for tracking progress on an orderly estate plan and ownership transfer. This is more easily attacked with outside, objective advisors. A family member pushing on either estate planning or passing down business ownership will come across as greedy, even if they have the best intentions. While this is not a board role for the normal business, it is a great task for your Board of Directors to tackle.

Term & Logistics

The shareholders can decide on the terms of service for board members. A common practice is three terms, with each term being two to three years in length. If you are just starting to set term limits, stagger the terms so only one-third of the board is rotating off at one time. Please don't overlook term limits—most board members have exhausted their ideas, advice, alliances, and partnership opportunities by the end of their second term. Holding onto them indefinitely is a disservice to the CEO and the business. Rotation brings in new energy, perspective, innovation, and oversight that all companies desperately need to stay competitive.

Compensation for board members is dependent on the size of the business, and data can be received from a compensation analyst. Generally it is structured as a retainer fee, along with a per meeting fee, plus travel expense coverage. Meetings are commonly held on a quarterly basis and scheduled for a year in advance.

Decision-making

The governance of the business usually begins with the founding parents. Decision-making is an on-going, informal meeting of Mom and Dad at work during the day and at the kitchen table during the evening. Please stop here and protect your bedroom from TV and business conversations.

As the business expands down into the second and third generation, it becomes important to structure officers of the board, bylaws, quorums, voting, and resolutions. The technical part of this can be quickly and easily agreed on. The challenging part is transitioning and keeping the board conversations and decisions at a strategic, not operational, level.

Many boards focus on operational decisions—software purchase for project management, the color of the new building, or the replacement of the receptionist with an automated phone system. These operational discussions strip the CEO and his team's ability to make fast, smart decisions. More important, it leads the board away from their task of providing strategic, high-level direction and insight.

Strategic discussions such as expanding to a new market, product diversification, and acquisition potentials will better support the CEO and the company. Are you asking the strategic questions and looking at the business's risk management practices, industry trends, demographics, product and service diversity, and company financial trends?

Board Challenges

The governance of the business—Annual Shareholder Meeting, Board of Directors, and Family Council—is crucial to being able to "pass the business, please." Why is Uncle John allowed to sit on the board and sleep through half of the meetings? When siblings and cousins don't trust each other to make the best business decision, sometimes there are board seats that are present just to protect turf. As a company matures, trust increases, the roles and responsibilities of the board are better understood, and the board moves from operational to strategic and financial oversight. If this is not happening, it's time to step back and bring in experts to help identify and fix the problem.

Family board membership should be based on ability to contribute, not on bloodline; insisting on representation by family spells trouble. As mentioned earlier, in a family of five siblings, it's common that each sibling would have one of their family members sitting on the board, regardless of their ability to provide value. This is definitely not ideal. The more you align your board to be professional and effective, the greater it will serve the company, employees, and family shareholders. A better family member selection process would be to say, "I want a total of seven board members—four will be outside experts, and three will be family members." Suppose there are six family bloodlines (six siblings in the second generation). Create a profile of the skills, abilities, and knowledge you are looking for, develop a board member job description, and distribute it widely to all family members. You could also ask for submissions and create a committee to review the family member board applications leading to a decision of the best three to serve.

Another common mistake is in the choice of the outside board members. Many a board member is recruited over a drink or during a golf game. You may choose someone you're comfortable with, such as an advisor you're already using—your CPA or attorney. But these people don't always have the expertise needed for board membership. Instead, look to industry experts, a past or currently practicing CFO of a company larger than your company, an industry innovator, a retired executive from your industry, and/or strategist. Go through a deliberative process of creating the ideal board member profile, and *then* seek out that person.

The most common challenge is to not form a board at all, or to form it and infrequently meet. Other challenges are confusing the responsibilities and decision levels between the Board of Directors, shareholders, Executive Leadership Team, CEO, and Family Council. The following graphic representation summarizes these governance roles.

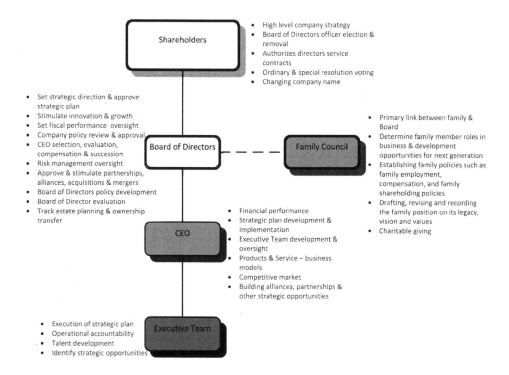

While high level strategy and financial performance is the board's usual role, at times they may need to take a more active role in operational oversight. This may occur during a company crisis, family crisis, or a significant external market threat. When a family has internal conflict between high level leaders (i.e. an uncle and nephew), the board may refocus the leadership team back to the customers' needs and away from a family turf war.

Please...Form a Family Council

What role does the Family Council play in governance of the business? The Family Council educates family members about the business, integrates the next generation into the business, and provides for family legacy. This forum can be an avenue to educate family on their options and responsibilities around buy-sell agreements, dividend distribution, a loan program, family office, wealth transfer, and individual financial planning.

Many CEOs, both family and non-family, complain about the interference of family members in the business. The Family Council gives family members a place to understand the direction, vision, and mission of the business while offering their input via their Family Council representative on the Board of Directors, without interfering at the CEO and management level. The Council helps everyone understand the difference between the role of shareholder, Board of Director member, Family Council member, company CEO, and company employee.

Membership of the Family Council varies from family to family. Some keep it limited to two or three representatives per bloodline; others invite everyone. The business that has structured and limited membership will usually sponsor a separate, annual family retreat that includes everyone—sometimes known as an Annual Family Assembly. Limiting the membership to bloodlines is generally not successful, as the spouses are intricately involved with their children, and will be less supportive and knowledgeable if they are not included in the family business activities. As generation two moves to generation three, creating committees to do work between Council meetings is helpful.

As families move from the third to the fourth generation, the overall size of the Family Council becomes hard to manage and many families may move to representatives from each family branch and limit the size of the Council. For example, if there were five children in generation two, those family branches might be represented by two or three people, resulting in a Family Council that is between ten and fifteen members. As the membership of the Family Council increases, the family may decide to use voting for critical decisions. Some Councils stay with consensus the entire time, while others set up a "one vote per family branch" system. Others require a super majority vote for key decisions.

Family Council meetings should be structured to fit your family. Some families meet as little as once a year and combine it with the annual Christmas or Thanksgiving holiday. Other family members meet three or four times each year for half day sessions. Some families take advantage of bringing the full family together to do half a day of work and a half day of play in a vacation setting.

Decision-making and voting is generally not a function of the Family Council. Conversations and education on important family matters, such as communication, coordinated estate planning, and individual financial planning, is perfect for a session. There are usually presentations by experts, including professional advisors, the CEO, and non-family managers. These non-family managers may keep the family informed by presenting new business technology and industry trends.

At the beginning, Councils are busy creating charters and codes of conduct, identifying values, creating policies, and setting a curriculum of education. As the Family Council develops and the business matures, many families will provide for personal financial planning and estate planning, knowing that financially independent family members allow the business to stay focused on strategy, not meeting individual family member demands. These structures for education and discussion, coupled with liquidity options, will support family harmony. The last thing you want to do is insist that all family members remain in the family business, either through financial investment or employment.

Some families use Council time to create a charitable family foundation. The younger generation works together to identify social issues, connect with community nonprofits, and make decisions on charitable donations. Other families volunteer together. These interactions serve a dual purpose—giving back to the community and strengthening family ties.

As mentioned, a typical Family Council meeting will include a brief company update from the CEO, education around the shareholder dividend program, a speaker on industry trends, a relationship building activity, and a report on the family foundation activities. Reading articles or a book in preparation for meetings helps engage and educate the family. Topic areas can include stockholder agreements, family employment, buy-sell agreements, individual financial planning, charitable giving, and estate planning. An outside facilitator allows all family members to participate fully, with the facilitator focusing on the process and family dynamics. This enables the family to focus on the meeting content. These meetings ultimately prepare the family to be good stewards of the business and family wealth.

There are times when Family Council formation is not suggested, such as if the family is in crisis or conflict, they have threatened or are suing each other, or there is a problem with substance abuse of key family members. These issues need to be addressed before moving forward.

One of the frequent objections to forming a Council is "we're too small." If there are two siblings in the second generation, a Family Council is appropriate—it is better to be proactive than reactive to family missteps with the business. The Council may only meet once or twice a year, but it is a great vehicle to begin to understand the business, agree on how family members should interact with the business, and agree on how to prepare the next generation. No matter how small the family is, getting into the habit of meeting, talking, and making decisions will lay a foundation of working together.

The Family Council proactively addresses conflict, educates the next generation on becoming a shareholder or employee, and prepares for effective wealth transfer. By generation three, it becomes obvious that good, ongoing communication between everyone is critical. At this point, you may need outside assistance to manage the meeting preparation and follow-up.

One of the first tasks of the Family Council is to create its charter or statement of purpose. The charter confirms the purpose of the Council, definition of family membership, roles, the structure and logistics of meetings, expense reimbursement, relationship to the family as a whole, the board and company Executive Management Team, charitable giving, rules of conduct, and how to amend the charter. Charters can also be a place to state family values and your collective commitment to the business legacy. The charter may acknowledge the Council's role of preparing the next generation, handling family grievances, holding healthy boundaries between governance groups, and promoting responsible business ownership.

While it's great to talk about the proactive development of the Council, its beginnings are usually steeped in family tension or conflict—a family member is perceived to be unfairly released from employment, someone needs money and has no way of tapping into their stock holdings, or some family members are unhappy with the recent non-family executive hire. Address the issue at hand, and then start the Council to head off future pain points.

Some Councils don't get off the ground because one branch of the family doesn't think that it's necessary or they want to tell their children, in their own way, about the business. This should not be an excuse to delay Council start-up; rather, it is confirmation that it is needed.

The Council will establish family guidelines or policies around employment, communication, and confidentiality. Some families also adopt a written philosophy, along with a policy and procedure for handling and resolving conflict. It is important to agree on the process to develop, review, edit, re-draft, approve, and ultimately implement, prior to the development of the first policy.

It is helpful to involve others in the Family Council workings. For example, the Chairman of the Board should review and understand the Family Charter, guidelines, and policies. The Chief Talent Officer or Human Resources Director can assist in arranging family education in areas such as communication and conflict resolution. The inclusion of others—shareholders, board members, company managers—with Family Council members will create mutual support and good will.

Ultimately the shareholders (owners) of the business will elect and evaluate the governance of the Board of Directors. The Family Council can serve as a forum for owners to bring themselves in alignment with each other's expectations of the business's performance from a perspective of investors.

There should be an ongoing discussion between the CEO, Family Council members, Board of Directors, and owners regarding the direction of the company. What is the philosophy of the owners? Slow growth with minimal debt and dependable annual returns to shareholders, or aggressive growth that's funded with medium to high debt and variable returns to the shareholders? Out of these conversations and a review of the company performance, the Family Council, owners, and Board of Directors can draft a distribution policy. Reaching a balance of strategy for capital expenditures, business strategy, and shareholder returns needs to be reviewed on an annual basis. These and other discussions about how the family can best contribute to the success of the business demonstrate the effectiveness of the governance structures. One of the best gifts a CEO can leave to the next generation is an effective governance structure.

La Tortilla Factory

When Carlos handed the CEO title to Stan Mead, a non-family executive, other governance structures changed. At that time, the Board of Directors was primarily in place to fulfill legal obligations. The governance decisions, up to that time, were met with Carlos, Willie, and Mike meeting at a local diner for breakfast, writing strategy and decisions on the back of napkins and legal pads. They would strategize sales needs and other company business to carry back to employees.

With the move of Carlos from CEO to Chairman of the Board, the board became active. Initially, the board included Carlos Tamayo, his son Sam Tamayo, Willie Tamayo, his son Andy Tamayo, and two open positions designated for outside directors. Carlos and his family thoughtfully looked for and filled those outside positions with people who could help them within their industry.

A Family Council has not been established at La Tortilla Factory. While Willie, Carlos' brother, continues to work in La Tortilla Factory, majority stock ownership rests with Carlos and his son, Sam Tamayo, who assumed CEO leadership in 2012. Carlos has had family meetings with Sam and his two sisters to discuss transfer of the business and estate planning. While these have been good, there have still been times when the structure and policies of a Council would have improved the relationships between family members. As with most family businesses, one of the most difficult areas that a Council could have helped is with understanding and agreeing on who will enter the business, who should report to whom, and what performance levels are acceptable via the creation of a Family Employment Guideline.

Lundberg Family Farms

Lundberg Family Farms has a governance system that includes an annual shareholder meeting, Board of Directors, and Family Council; they actually have two boards—one for the company, Lundberg Family Farms, and one that provides oversight and direction for the farmland operations.

Their governance structures have evolved. When Grant stepped into the CEO role, the board was more operational, and Grant's executive team involved approximately 14 direct reports. Over time, Grant was clear about how ineffective both structures were (the Board of Directors and the large internal executive team). The board became more strategic in their deliberations, and Grant was given the go-ahead to trim his team to five direct reports. Bryce, Harlan's son, noted that the current nine-member Board is good for reaching decisions, and that there were times, in the beginning of the business, that they let opportunities slip by because of the decision by full inclusion process. The board has just added an independent, outside director this past year and they are looking for a second one.

While their Family Council is relatively young, at three years, there is enthusiastic support of how it is bringing the fourth generation together in support of family business legacy. Some of the third generation noted that they feel like the fourth generation will be better prepared as employees or for governance roles because of the Council's involvement. The third generation took about nine months deciding on the purpose and structure of the Council, wanting to be sure that they built the trust between fourth generation family members while increasing their knowledge about the business. Jennifer Parrish, third generation, noted that while her father, Eldon, worked daily with his three brothers, the next generation of cousins were more scattered, and therefore, didn't develop those close connections. The Council is beginning to fill in that gap and prepare the next generation for employment, leadership, and governance. The Council is also currently working on a family employment policy.

The family is heavily involved in both governance and employment at Lundberg. Family employees include Bryce Lundberg, Grant Lundberg, Jessica Lundberg, Tim Schultz, Jordan Schultz, Anders Lundberg, Joe Lundberg, and Eric Lundberg; family on the Board of Directors include Mark Lundberg (Chair of the Board), Bryce Lundberg, Alysicia Lundberg, Kevin Parrish, Grant Lundberg, Jessica Lundberg, Tim Schultz, and Kent Lundberg.

Lundberg has been thoughtful about the development of their governance structure, and have invested in the development and maintenance of these bodies.

Interiors Unlimited

Neal's Board of Directors at Interiors Unlimited was an annual meeting to look at the company performance and decide on the bonuses for the top three people—himself, his son Tom, and his stepson Don. Their Board of Directors was the legally required annual officer meeting. There was no evaluation of the CEO, input into the strategic direction of the company, or open look at the financials of Interiors Unlimited and N & R Supplies. The meeting was conducted at their external company attorney's office and lasted about an hour.

Development of a Family Council or objective Board of Directors was not a consideration for Neal. When raised as a potential idea, his response was a hearty laugh. He and his wife owned all of the shares, and when he started selling shares to his son and stepson, he did a regular dance of retracting his offer, forcing them to relinquish shares back to him.

*   *   *   *   *

Commitment and discipline are required to develop an effective governance structure. Thoughtfulness, linkage, and transparency are crucial to the effective functioning of the internal company executive management team, the Board of Directors, shareholders, and Family Council. The rewards make the effort worthy—preparation and engagement of the next generation, product innovation, better execution of plans, a greater likelihood of longevity, employee satisfaction, and family harmony.

Questions for Chapter 5 – Who's at the Head of the Table: Family Business Governance:

1. How would you describe the current level of functioning of your Board of Directors?

2. How is the membership of your Board of Directors determined?

3. How do you prepare owners for the Annual Shareholder Meeting?

4. How would you describe the role of your Family Council?

5. How is membership for the Family Council determined?

6. How often does the Family Council meet and how is the meeting agenda constructed?

7. How do the CEO, Board of Directors, shareholders, and Family Council interact?

8. What success story can you tell about your governance structure?

9. What changes would you like to see with your governance structure?

"He who every morning plans the transactions of that day and follows that plan carries a thread that will guide him through the labyrinth of the most busy life."

–VICTOR HUGO

CHAPTER 6
WHO IS PASSING WHAT?
PLANNING RULES

The discipline of planning differentiates any company, not just a family-owned business.

Do you have processes and structures to encourage the next generation's focus on being entrepreneurial? Is there a family venture seed fund, an incubator, or online family forum? Is there a separate holding company where a new business idea can be tried? Are business plans encouraged before entry into the family business?

Any successful business plans. In fact, their processes and structures are imbedded with on-going planning. Their leadership team and managers are well-trained in planning and process improvement, and they are disciplined in tracking their goals.

Areas for planning include:

1. Sudden death (contingency plan for the business and buy-sell agreement; key person life insurance)

2. Disability (disability insurance)

3. Retirement (financial plan)

4. Business plan (business plan, strategic plan, business transfer)

5. Leadership (management succession plan development, implementation and review)

6. Transfer of wealth to the next generation (ownership succession and estate plan)

Succession frequently fails or falters when one or more key family leaders do not adequately plan for their retirement. Their lifestyle will not be supported by their savings and they begin stretching their departure from the family business because they need the cash flow from their salary. There are conservative leaders who prepare early so that by the time they're 45 to 50 they are financially ready for retirement and confident about passing the business to the next generation. Unfortunately, I have seen many leaders who have either had to reinvest a lot of their own personal wealth back into the business to survive a downturn or have a lifestyle larger than their means without an adequate retirement, even if they keep working until they're 80.

Business Planning

The strategic plan is usually developed by the CEO and her team. The draft strategic plan is then presented to the Board of Directors for review, change, and approval. This is the guiding document for growth, diversity, and market share goals for the company. The board and executive team also need to develop contingency plans in case of disability or death of a key employee along with succession planning for these employees.

The other critical part of business planning is the transition plan. The owner and family's desire to either transfer the business to the next generation, seek other investors, and/or prepare for a sale should be discussed on an annual basis. Whether these discussions occur at the Board of Directors meeting or the Family Council doesn't matter as long as it is written down, acted on, and reviewed. Being clear about the direction that the business is headed and communicating this to the Board of Directors, Family Council, and company executive team will keep everyone aligned.

Strategic planning encourages growth and sustainability, leading to job creation, further wealth, and family harmony. Planning reconfirms the vision of the company, presents opportunities for product and service diversity, and stimulates innovation. Looking five to ten years in the future and matching family growth to company growth is crucial. Like any other company, the family business needs to build their competitive advantage, adaptability, and innovation. The business's edge can come from financial resources, physical assets, brand equity, talent pool, systems, processes, and distribution system. The ability of the family business to reach and retain customers, because of the family, can be an advantage in the marketplace. Still some families unknowingly rely on their perception of the customers experience versus doing good focus group research. While the family name can produce value, being family-owned will not cover the sins of poor or wrong products and services.

Diligently applied planning increases profitability and sustainability. Few things bring on family conflict faster than declining dividends and inadequate compensation. It can also start a cycle of poor employee morale, resulting in increased turnover. When cash flow and reserves are good, the family tends to be satisfied with pursuing their own outside interests. If profit begins to dwindle, family members, who have depended on dividends or distributions as income versus discretionary spending, grab for a share of the shrinking pie.

The next step in planning is for CEO succession and leadership continuity. Succession in any company is an on-going process of continually developing and stretching people in key positions. This may include assignments in different functional areas, difficult projects with mentors, association with professional groups, training, education, and executive coaching. Business transition planning increases family harmony. The planning opens up channels of communication between company management, the board, Family Council, and other family members. It signals certainty around a leadership shift to the next generation.

While succession and continuity considers a planned transition for leadership in the future, contingency planning is the proverbial answer to "what do we do if the CEO gets hit by a bus tomorrow?" This can be a simple two-page document with an organizational chart identifying the top five to eight critical positions in the company and detailing who and how they will step in. After the initial contingency plan is created, an annual look and revision should be on the CEO's calendar.

Wealth Transfer Planning

The philosophy of money management and transfer of wealth varies from family to family. Some owners will skip their children and transfer the bulk of their wealth to their grandchildren; others transfer to children only; and still others will give most of their estate to charity. One sibling in generation two may gift their company stock, while their two siblings will want or need to sell their stock to their children.

The complexity of estate planning and tax consequences demands considerable energy. Finding advisors—CPA, estate planning attorney, and certified financial planner—who are professional, experienced, and highly skilled takes time. Unfortunately, there are examples of attorneys and CPAs who stray into areas outside of their expertise and create plans and wealth transfer scenarios that at best don't serve the family well and at worst may financially harm them.

Talk to the clients of prospective advisors, check out credentials, look at several candidates for each area of expertise, and ask about their firm's plan for succession. Who will your children be working with thirty years from now? Do a thorough interview process, and when the estate plan is complete, consider a second look by another team of professionals. Your planning will only be as strong as the weakest advisor. An advisor that was ideal when you started your business may not be prepared for the long haul. Also consider appointing a lead for your advisor team, someone with the knowledge and experience level to coordinate everyone through the planning process.

A comprehensive estate plan looks at the allocation of income sources to the founder, his or her spouse, and active and non-active family members, as well as their heirs. It also addresses who will control the business. Some families get stuck here with parents trying to treat their children fairly by gifting shares equally. These trust arrangements may be difficult to administer and will sometimes leave control of the company to multiple children. While the parents desire to treat everyone as equals is understandable, one or two children working in the business may be left with the burden of making decisions that the parents should have made. The siblings working in the business will likely have to deal with their non-working siblings. These non-working siblings may insert themselves into business decisions based on their own personal interests, instead of what is best for the business.

For example, if capital is needed for new equipment, this could decrease quarterly dividends to shareholders, something that may be supported by the working siblings but not the siblings that are distanced from daily operations. If the current generation of owners do not transition to the next generation—by not transferring voting stock at the appropriate time or by requiring that important decisions be made by multiple shareholders who have equal amounts of stock—the business could falter or fail.

Why Plan?

It's not fun, it's expensive, but it's necessary. Families who have not planned with a buy-sell agreement, contingency plan, succession plan, life insurance coverage, disability insurance, and other wealth and management transition strategies find themselves more vulnerable to the ups and downs of business.

Planning leads to healthy conversations about what's important to the family, such as:

- What amount do we invest back into the business, to ourselves, to employees, the community?

- When do we gift to our children?

- Does it include the ability to vote on business decisions now?

- How have we planned for tax consequences? For retirement?

- Do we gift stock to our children, or do they purchase stock?
- Do we gift stock to children working in the business and make other transfers of wealth to children not in the business?
- What are our siblings doing and how might that impact us?

Hopefully these dialogues and diligent planning will avert future conflict between family members and between the family and the business.

Planning will help you better understand how the owners are going to exit, and how the next generation will step up to wealth management and company leadership. It will give you time to consider if you want to treat the business as a family legacy or as an asset to prepare for an internal or external sale.

Planning can include rewarding non-family key executives to encourage them to stay and build company value. When stock is not an option, planning can include many different methods including Phantom Stock, Warrants or Options, Stock Appreciation Right programs or Non-Qualified Retirement Plans.

Unfortunately, many owners and family members have not done the level of planning needed to realize an orderly exit or succession of the business. When this happens, a disability or death of the family CEO can force rapid decisions that leave the company and family vulnerable.

La Tortilla Factory

Carlos remembers an early turning point in the family business that involved planning for their future. At the time, Carlos, Willie, Mike, their mother (Mary), and father (Jose) were maintaining a restaurant, retail store, and tortilla production and distribution. Carlos knew they had reached a tipping point. They were working hard and not really moving forward. They needed to change, but struggled with what that change should be. Their brothers, Tico and Bernie, were also covering the multiple small businesses on odd weekends to give the rest of the family a break. Carlos, Willie, Mary, and Jose met with a management consultant in San Francisco who helped them reach the conclusion that they needed to focus on one area and do that well. Tortillas became their specialty.

This marked two different attributes that has led to business sustainability—their dedication to planning and the use of outside expertise. Their willingness to take a step back, reflect, and plan, coupled with the discipline to execute, has served them well into the third generation.

Lundberg Family Farms

Planning, conversation, and consensus are in the DNA structure of the Lundberg family. The original four brothers—Eldon, Wendell, Harlan, and Homer—consistently met twice a week to discuss and coordinate their areas of function within the business. From the beginning, the family looked for best practices in business and in rice production. They were not only open to outside influence and ideas, but also actively sought it. Planning was and is central to their way of working together.

Internally, they actively listen to each other. Homer, one of the four original brothers, noted that each family member is involved in planning and innovation. They will come up with something new and "we will listen to their ideas and try it out."

They practice conservative money management, both in the business and in their individual families. They have invested wisely, and consistently include everyone's input with decisions that will have a big impact on the business and family. They have been thoughtful about both planning and the transfer of wealth. Homer, the youngest brother from the second generation, noted that not one of the family members owns a second vacation home. They live comfortably, but not extravagantly, and are conscientious about the need to reinvest in the business and in employees.

Interiors Unlimited

Planning at Interiors Unlimited occurred in Neal's head and wasn't written or communicated to the rest of the company or family. He did several strategic things early on, such as adding N & R Supplies as an additional source of revenue that was linked to Interiors Unlimited needs. When it came time for Neal to retire, wealth and business transition was again kept close to his chest and not discussed with his son and stepson. When planning discussions did arise, Neal took the lead, telling family members what would happen. He proudly asserted that his dominant leadership style could be summed up as "it's my way or the highway."

Questions for Chapter 6 – Who is Passing What? Planning Rules:

1. Can you describe the different types of planning you do as a business?

2. What type of outside expertise have you used in planning? How did you decide on these experts?

3. What is your family's philosophy around the transfer of wealth to the next generation?

4. What progress have you made in estate planning?

5. When did you last have your advisors review your estate plan?

6. Have you made provisions for one person to have the majority voting control in the next generation?

7. How would you describe your current readiness for retirement (from a financial perspective)?

8. What area of planning could use more focus?

"My dear young cousin, if there's one thing I've learned over the eons, it's that you can't give up on your family, no matter how tempting they make it."
–RICK RIORDAN

CHAPTER 7
KEEPING EVERYONE
AT THE TABLE HEALTHY
AND HAPPY

Alll families have their proverbial warts—free floating anxiety or the uncle who is the center of concern and conversation. Preserving your family begins with an assessment of your current state of health and where it needs to be in order to support a legacy business. When you can honestly look at your family and your role in it, you will be able to put your strengths to use and bring in other talent to cover your weaknesses. The healthier the family is, the greater your ability to take inventory of these strengths and weaknesses.

Globally speaking, the more skilled a family is at supporting each other's individuality and development, the greater likelihood there is of peace and business success. A family with high anxiety levels, emotional dependence on one another, substance abuse, and multiple divorces has the odds stacked against them. Tack on outside factors like frequent market fluctuations, rapidly changing market desires, and tightened capital, and the combined external and internal stresses can push any family over the edge.

So where to start? Carlos (La Tortilla Factory), Tom (Interiors Unlimited), and Grant (Lundberg Family Farms) all attribute a large portion of their family and personal successes to a belief in and ethical practice of something bigger than themselves. As Carlos explained : *"God places dreams in the minds of visionary people. He tells them what to do, but He does not tell them how to do it."* Tom went through a challenging period in his twenties that led him to a higher power and practice based on Alcoholics Anonymous principles that he still leans on. The Lundberg family has been actively involved in the Richvale Evangelical Free Church. Digging deeper into their organizations, you will note these beliefs and personal practices reflected in their ethical treatment of customers and employees.

This is not to say that a belief in God or practice of religion is the cornerstone. In this example, it was a theme that was mentioned by the three business stories we are following. As mentioned earlier, one of the younger Lundberg family members noted that even if they weren't actively practicing in the church, it was simply assumed they were, but they weren't pushed either way. What they were held responsible for was their honesty and hard work—and this is clear throughout the company. A quick look at their website shares their honest conversations with customers about GMO (genetically modified organisms) and labeling of food products.

Knowing what is expected of each other and of employees provides a sense of security and belonging that decreases stress and anxiety. These closely held family values and beliefs can and do support the health of a family. They also provide a strong, ongoing guideline for acceptable behavior. These values are strengthened by family employees consistently doing what they say they believe.

Let's move on to our motives, intentions, and experience as a family in business together.

Motives, Intentions, and Experience

Are your brothers, sisters, and cousins motivated to reinvest money back into the business? Is the intent for personal gain, family harmony, business longevity, or a sale of the business? Has their experience been one of strong attachment or resentment?

The motives and intentions of the first generation are relatively simple, and are often driven by one person and their spouse. The next generation begins to include the first generation's children, their spouses, and their kids. The third generation adds cousins, more spouses, aging parents, and a new generation of children. Each layer increases the number of people and the resulting matrix of relationships. Now you are not the generation raised by the same two parents under one roof, but possibly five sets of parents with differing values and experiences.

Even the second generation can have a different experience with the same two parents. Older siblings may remember a very different father than the younger siblings remember. Older siblings may also hold deep resentments against their father because he was focused more on the business than them, and in turn may resent the business itself. Younger siblings may have had more of their father's time. Now into generation three, new bloodlines raised in different homes cause the experiences and resulting motives and intentions to be even further apart.

An honest discussion about what each family member expects from the business is frequently not approached. Knowing the motives and intentions to either sell or grow the business will help the Board of Directors and the business align with the family's vision. These dialogues are frequently emotional and complicated, and are facilitated by using an objective, experienced advisor who understands family business. It can also be supported by a thoughtful, non-family board member.

Relationship Building

Building relationships within and between generations is crucial for long-term family health and business success. Relationships strengthen the sense of belonging and increase your commitment to each other. Your relationships, when nurturing and supportive, lead to personal fulfillment and creative energy. When relationships are destructive, there is a feeling of alienation, fear, and distrust that mounts and overshadows any desire to build something together. You have likely experienced both types of relationship "building" in your life, and those that nurture and support you also support the business.

Lundberg Family Farms has identified the importance of relationships within the family and, specifically, within a growing fourth generation (G4) by recently creating the "Boot Camp." Cousins from their late teens to mid-20s gather for a long weekend during the summer to learn about the business, but more important, to get to know themselves and each other better. While most of the family still resides in northern California, one of the cousins from Tennessee participated last year. The news of the G4 Boot Camp success spread quickly throughout the family, leaving some G3 family members wishing they were given a similar opportunity for meaningful connection.

The original four Lundberg brothers intuitively understood the importance of including everyone, developing individuals, and building family relationships. Several members of the third generation noted that attending family gatherings as kids included their grandfather or uncle asking them to stand up and talk about what they were doing. This also occurred if they were sitting in on one of the weekly business meetings that took place at the local Richvale Café. One of the four brothers would ask them to stand and share how they were doing in school, or what traveling they had done recently, or simply talk about something they were interested in. Though sometimes embarrassing, this practice taught them many things including how to present in front of others, how to include others, and how to be supportive of each other.

Emma, Grant's daughter, noted that it is part of their family DNA to ask for everyone's input and to be overachievers. While Emma doesn't see herself working in the business, because of her career focus on music, she is obviously passionate about the family business legacy.

Building relationships takes time, acknowledgement, care, and respect. Providing opportunities to work, talk, and play together is essential for family relationships to develop. The advent of electronic and remote communication is making this more doable, but face time is still important. Most families have noted a lack of time as a significant barrier. One strategy is to combine a family business meeting along with an already planned family gathering, such as birthday celebrations or holidays. I'm guessing it wouldn't be smart, but maybe funny and interesting, to try to tack a Family Council meeting on to a wedding.

As with any relationship, trust is the cornerstone. Therefore, doing what you say you will do and practicing transparency within the business and your family interactions is crucial. One of the common causes of distrust is lack of transparency. Even when nothing illegal or fattening is occurring, in the absence of knowing, people will fill in the blanks with a story that does not build good will.

As the family expands in number, it becomes more important to carve out time for interaction. This interaction can be attending social events together, sharing a meal, or working on a project together. One family may work together on a Habitat for Humanity project, while another may gather for a monthly birthday celebration. When Family Council events are planned primarily around business education, allow space for "getting to know you" activities throughout the meeting day.

One of the ways to jump start a family discussion on relationships is to use a relationship assessment. Rank the family with one being low and ten being high in the following assessment and start a conversation about where your family relationships are strong and where they could use some bolstering.

Relationship Awareness©

	Challenged to	Healthy	Rank
Personality & Communication Style	Stubborn, poor communication skills, closed, antisocial, antagonistic, withholding and rigid	Open, connected, empathetic, giving and agile; good communication skills	
Motive & Intention	Attacks to look better than the 'other person'; puts self before and above others	Relates and collaborates with others; puts others before self	
Trust	Frequently doesn't do what they promise; lack of ethics and character	Consistently does what they say they will do; supports others; has high ethical standards and good character	
Sense of Self (ego)	Self-doubt and self-centered	Healthy sense of self and others	
Connection	Lack of connection with others	Well connected to others	
Boundaries	Shows extremes of either rigid boundaries, or is inappropriately all inclusive	Flexible, appropriate and clear	
Emotions	Exhibits high anxiety, emotional distress, psychic pain, jealousy, fear and disconnect; reactive versus thoughtful; bouts of anger and drama	Has healthy handling of anxiety, sense of well-being, calm and rational; confidence and connection; expresses emotions but thinks before reacting	
Introspective	Unaware of how their behavior affects others; thinks the other person needs to change; defensive to feedback and refuses to change behavior	Reflective of own behavior and able to accommodate and adjust to others; understands and owns their part in the relationship; accepts feedback and changes behavior	
			Total Score

Family Education

Unless there is pain, high anxiety, or a symptom (i.e. Uncle Joe is drinking again, Mia Tia Maria is on yet another shopping spree, Dad is on an anger rampage), families don't think about training or facilitated discussions. Let's face it…it's a rare family who actually meets once a week, and many have slipped from sharing an evening meal together.

Here are seven training areas that proactively build family health:

1. Understanding family systems

2. Communication skills

3. Conflict mediation

4. Relationship development

5. Effective parenting skills

6. Personal money management

7. Business and governance best practices

Ideally, each of these topics is covered during a three-hour session, followed a few weeks later with a two-hour discussion. My experience is that many families initially express a loud, clear "No!" to this joint learning, and then embrace it as one of the primary reasons for their success. When you step back and think about it, though, you likely spend approximately 1,800 hours a year interacting with your family, yet you probably have little to no training or role models on how to do it well. Still, the expectation is that it will go smoothly!

Imagine someone saying, "I want to be the Chief Financial Officer of your business but I don't have a finance or accounting degree from college, I don't have bookkeeper experience, I haven't learned about accounting principles, and I haven't worked as a controller in another business. Oh, but I love numbers!" You would fall over laughing. But the point is simple: most people rarely invest time to acquire the knowledge and skills needed to have a healthy family. In reality, if you take the time to try, it may well be the best investment you ever make.

Family Council

You may be thinking, *are we really talking about this again?* Yes! It is always worth the time and energy. If started early in the history of the business, family meetings provide a vehicle for everyone to better understand the benefits and responsibilities of owning a business. It is also a forum to proactively reduce conflict, clear up misconceptions, and avert resentments.

Family Council meetings, minimally scheduled twice a year, will educate family members about the business while building relationships. Communicating what each family member can and cannot expect from the business sets the tone for the family. A sense of entitlement is hopefully diminished as each family member understands their role and responsibility to the business, to employees, and to each other.

Again, Family Council meetings should begin early in the history of the business. A common challenge is waiting too long to begin a Family Council. Repeated requests for personal loans from the company, grumbling about dwindling dividends, and guesses about the financial realities of the business build into conflict and resentment, destroying relationships as the pile of grievances grow. The consistent and thoughtful conduct of family meetings should be valued just as governance of the business is valued through the formation of the Board of Directors.

Many family members will wear two or even three hats in the family and business and, therefore, need a forum to discuss how they should interact in each role. I may be a mother, an aunt, a spouse to the Chief Operating Officer (COO), a member of the Family Council, a shareholder, and sit on the Board of Directors. When do I interact as a Board of Director member, as Mom, or as a coach to the Chief Operating Officer, my husband? It's easy to see the need for a forum for discussion about these multiple roles and their related responsibilities.

A starting point for developing the Family Council is building a charter or statement of purpose and developing a family code of conduct. Some families also work on identifying their top values and beliefs that they hold as a family and a business. Family Council meetings can be a place to learn about the business, strategic planning, business risk management, ownership, buy-sell agreements, financial statements, dividends, capital expenditures, and industry trends.

As the family grows, managing sibling, cousins, and spouse relationships becomes more difficult. A family map, with frequent updates, is a visual way to keep track and feel connected. This genealogy can be color coded to indicate who is working in the business, is a part of the Board of Directors, participates in Family Council, and/or is a Shareholder. Some families put birthdates, their top three skills or abilities, and where they live. This helps new spouses get to know the family and is a way to connect with the company's executive management team.

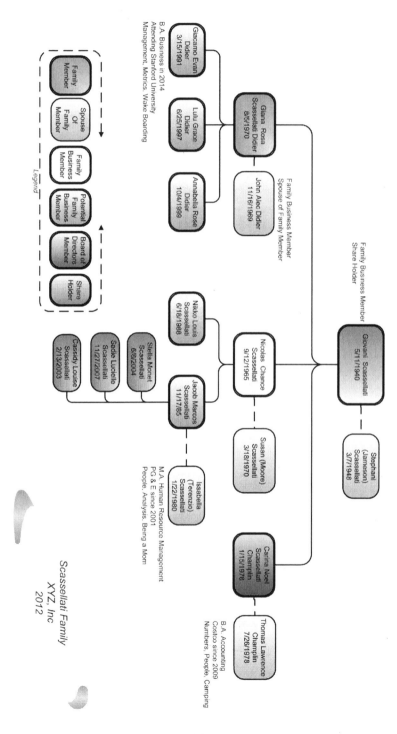

Giacamo Evan Didier
3/15/1991

B.A. Business in 2014
Attending Stanford University
Management, Metrics, Wake Boarding

Giana Rosa Scassellati Didier
8/5/1970

Lulu Grace Didier
6/25/1997

Annabella Rose Didier
10/4/1999

John Alec Didier
11/16/1969

Family Business Member
Spouse of Family Member

Family Business Member
Share Holder

Giovani Scassellati
5/11/1940

Stephani (Jameson) Scassellati
3/7/1948

Nikko Louis Scassellati
6/18/1988

Nicolas Chance Scassellati
9/12/1965

Susan (Moore) Scassellati
3/18/1970

Jacob Marcos Scassellati
11/17/85

Stella Monet Scassellati
6/8/2004

Sadie Luclelle Scassellati
11/27/2007

Cassidy Louise Scassellati
2/13/2003

Issabella (Terenzo) Scassellati
1/22/1980

M.A. Human Resource Management
PG & E since 2001
People, Analysis, Being a Mom

Carina Noel Scassellati Champlin
1/15/1978

Thomas Lawrence Champlin
7/26/1978

B.A. Accounting
Costco since 2009
Numbers, People, Camping

Legend

Family Member

Spouse Of Family Member

Family Business Member

Potential Family Business Member

Board of Directors Member

Share Holder

Scassellati Family
XYZ, Inc
2012

Managing Sibling and Cousin Rivalries

Treating shareholders, siblings, and cousins fairly does not mean equal treatment. Too many parents divide both shares and voting rights equally, leaving the kingdom without a ruling king or queen. The hope is that this power of the deciding vote is rarely, if ever, used.

What do you do with the competition, bullying, dominant, and passive behaviors? Sibling rivalry, from an evolutionary view, can positively increase the chances of survival to the next generation. Children naturally vie for their parents' attention and love, feel out the hierarchy of power, and in the process develop their perspective on the fairness of their parents' attention. *"Why does Mom let Jennifer slip by on homework and curfew?* turns into *"Why did Dad offer Jennifer the CEO position?"* The favoring of one sibling over another may occur because another sibling lives geographically closer, has accomplishments that are important to the parent, their personalities are similar to the parent, they have similar interests and hobbies, or there are grandchildren involved.

As an adult sibling who feels that one or both of your parents is unjustly favoring another sibling over you, you may cope by:

1. Gaining support and acknowledgement from other family members, friends, and colleagues

2. Focusing more on building your relationship with your siblings

3. Not taking it personally

4. Not competing with your siblings for your parents' love and approval

5. Accepting what is

6. Investing time and energy into your own family and friends

If you're a parent, you can take care to not overtly favor one child over another. You can also clearly identify why one adult child is chosen over another for business leadership, or better yet, bring in an objective, professional advisor to quantify which sibling and/or non-family member is the best choice for the position.

Sibling rivalry often means people verbally lash out before thinking, which leads us to the next skill we all need to have in our toolbox—forgiveness.

Forgiveness

Who has a company credit card? Was the cruise with clients more vacation than work? Who gets their gasoline paid for? How did Sally get into the accounting department without an interview?

As the number of family employees grows, so do resentments and grievances. Transparency, good communication skills, and a process for handling conflict will proactively develop relationships. Transparency with financial statements, business valuation, dividend distribution, and salaries is key. Also, clear company operating policies and procedures helps set and keep expectations in check. The more consistent you are in enforcing these policies, the higher likelihood you have of diverting conflict and improving relationships.

While men generally tend to forgive and forget faster than women, both men and women can play the role of victim equally well. The more undifferentiated and enmeshed a family is in each other's business, the more anxiety, grievances, and resentments pile up. A developmentally healthy family encourages individuation of each family member so that they utilize their talents and abilities in a supportive environment. This family is clear about boundaries. As adult children mature and branch out to college, career, and relationships, they are allowed to fail, succeed, and learn with little interference from their parents.

If you step over the line and are the cause of offending a family member (unlikely, I know), a quick and sincere "I'm sorry" and action to repair the "wrong" will serve you well. If family grievances, resentments, gossiping, and stuffing emotions are common, then good luck. You're going to need a process and a professional to untangle poor communication and relationship patterns.

We Love You, But....

What do you do when Uncle Arthur shows up to the Board of Directors meeting drunk? When Jim wants to drive a company truck, but has two DUIs? When Jean's moods and yelling cause high turnover in her department? We often forget to ask each other, as family members, if we would tolerate or ignore the same behavior in a non-family employee.

Developing a family guideline and process in the Family Council to address family members who may need training, therapy, rehab, or support is ideally done before problems are encountered. Understandably, families struggle with these conversations. Difficult or not, conversations and action need to occur. Bad behavior in the workplace can put the business at risk, so you can't afford to ignore poor family behaviors.

Clarifying beliefs and values early on will help the family intervene sooner. Also, one of the upsides of the family business is that there is frequently the financial ability to help each other if rehab and therapy are needed. If the offending behavior is not your family branch, seek out an approachable and respected family member from that branch and/or a professional to help strategize an approach.

Ideally, the Family Council will work at both educating family members on how to mediate conflict and develop a policy on how to handle it. When emotions are high, it is helpful to have these skills and written processes already in place.

La Tortilla Factory

In the early years, Alayne, Carlos' wife, remembers long hours home alone raising small children, while Carlos worked with his parents and brothers at the store. She would infrequently pitch in at the workplace, plunking her son, Sam (current CEO), on top of a pile of corn masa bags while she helped package tortillas. Alayne also recalls Sam calling the store "Dad's house" when he was three because of how much time was spent there. While the beginning years were tough, the brothers, nieces, and nephews stepped in to help. And while the family grew close from shared experience, the brothers were also fiercely independent in the areas they covered in the business.

Carlos found that while there was some push back and resentment, being the majority shareholder allowed the business to become the family legacy that he and his parents intended. While relationships between him and his brothers became strained during times of business transition and stock purchases, these transitions gave family members options.

For example, Mike, the youngest brother, was able to open a successful Mexican restaurant in Novato, California. They were able to financially help their brother Bernie and his family when he was losing his battle with cancer.

Simply struggling through the conversations of who should or shouldn't be in the business and where their talents were best placed has led to a deeper understanding of each other than most family's experience. Currently, Carlos' son, Sam, is the Chief Executive Officer; his daughter, Jenny, is working part-time as a social media manager; his brother Willie moved from the role of VP of Sales and Marketing to the Board of Directors as Secretary and Executive Vice President; and his nephew, Tomas Tamayo (Tico's son), entered the family business after his graduation from the University of California, Davis. He has been working in the family business for the past eight years in the sales department as a National Sales Account Executive. Tomas is currently working as a route sales representative in an effort to round out his work experience. He is a well-thought-of young man on a career path leading to a potential leadership position. Carlos' other nephew, Andy Tamayo (Willie's son), chose to work outside the family business after graduating from the University of California, Berkeley. Today, Andy is a highly regarded and successful young financial executive with a major Wall Street firm in San Francisco. In 2009, Andy was appointed to the Board of Directors and serves as the chair of the board's finance committee. Andy's outside corporate financial experience, knowledge of the family culture, and strategic thinking ability make him a valued director. Over the years, a dozen family members have worked in the business.

Lundberg Family Farms

Homer, the youngest brother of the second generation, noted that while the four brothers were all strong individuals with different ideas, they considered the spirit of "getting along" as the most important element within their family. An attitude of love and cooperation permeates their relationships, and while not perfect, they strive to understand and listen to both family and non-family in a respectful manner. While starkly honest communication is not encouraged because of the possibility of offending another, long and thoughtful discussions are common and are frequently rolled into a committee format when the decision may impact the business, family, or employees.

The third generation of Lundbergs formed a Family Council about three years ago to ensure family members continue to be connected and well-educated about the business. The Council meets six times a year and has been successful in bringing them together to understand their roles as family members, employees, and shareholders. The Council also sponsors two or three family social gatherings a year. They have also seriously embarked on preparing the next generation for leadership, governance, and stewardship of both the family and the business.

Interiors Unlimited

Neal went out of his way to ensure that people didn't trust each other—purposefully pitting one employee against another and even brother against stepbrother. Employees walked on eggshells, not knowing if they would have their position tomorrow. The business was "sold" to the brother and stepbrother and then yanked back several times. Relationships could best be described as adversarial, accusatory, and threatening. Tom recalls that when he lived at home during a college break, his dad accused him of "taking my pills," a stash that Neal had for keeping himself awake during long working days. Tom was not the culprit, but that is how communication occurred. Blaming and accusations trumped fact finding or open dialogue.

Questions for Chapter 7 – Keeping Everyone at the Table Healthy and Happy:

1. What would you list as your family's top five strengths?

2. What would you list as your family's top two weaknesses?

3. What part does God, religion, and/or ethics play in your experience of your family?

4. What would you note as your family's values and beliefs?

5. What type of training, if any, has been done with family members—communication, parenting, money management, etc.?

6. What training do you think your family would benefit from?

7. How would you describe your relationship with each of your siblings? Cousins? Aunts? Uncles? Parents?

8. How frequently does the second, third or fourth generation get together? How do they stay connected between these meetings?

9. How does the family manage problem behavior(s)?

10. How does the family manage conflict?

"Always bear in mind that your own resolution to succeed is more important than any one thing."

—ABRAHAM LINCOLN

CHAPTER 8

BUILDING BUSINESS SUSTAINABILITY

The CEO Exit

Is Uncle Dave going to let go of the business or is he just going to mention it again at the annual shareholder meeting? Smart CEOs of family businesses care more about the mission of the company and its continuity than their own egos or agendas. They understand that the business has a life beyond their individual position and that they are servants of a legacy. This CEO is always looking for and mentoring the next person who could fill their role. Not only does the CEO look at the sustainability of the business and the transition from one leader to the next, he or she also focuses on the development of an integrated estate plan to protect family wealth. Their next role is generally one of Board of Director leadership, ensuring that the governance of the business brings long-term value.

While family CEOs are generally in their position longer than a non-family business CEO (seventeen to twenty years versus six to eight years), there are many theories as to why this happens. Some theorize that family CEOs can stay regardless of results, while others strongly argue that CEOs of family businesses are more focused on sustainability and continuity of the business and are therefore encouraged to stay at the Board of Directors prompting. If the tenure of the CEO becomes even longer, 25 to 30 years, there are hidden costs of business stagnation, underutilized family leadership talent, and ultimately, family harmony begins to break down as the next generation is denied access to the president and vice president levels of leadership.

If the current CEO is ready to retire and the next potential family CEO is too young to lead the company, the company may begin a search for a bridge CEO—a non-family CEO who serves for a specific time until the next generation is prepared for leadership. This is a difficult move, yet it can be a great solution.

Even when a bridge CEO is appropriate, family businesses rarely look for an external candidate. By the time Stan Mead, non-family CEO at La Tortilla Factory, was tapped to be a bridge between Carlos Tamayo and his son, Sam, Stan was a trusted executive. Stan had served for about six years as their CFO, and before that he was their acting CFO as a consultant for another six years. These CEOs are often not considered "external" because they have worked with the company for ten to fifteen years, know the family dynamics, and are an integral part of the company culture. In fact, Carlos credits Stan Mead for his major contributions to the growth and profitability of the company and for training, mentoring, and coaching Sam Tamayo to become the third generation family CEO of the company.

The non-family CEO may not be just a bridge, but a long-term solution for a business that has outgrown the skills, abilities, and experience of the current generation. While many potential leaders of the next generation may prepare for the CEO position, some choose to serve as second in command, serve in a governance role, or leave the company entirely. Also, many adult children of the next generation admit to feeling pressured into taking a leadership role that doesn't match their skills or desire. As one CEO told me:

> *"After ten long years, I turned around and looked at myself leading in an industry that I wasn't passionate about...I felt trapped. I thought I was obligated to help my family and felt heavy guilt when I stepped down from the CEO role. I finally admitted that I wanted to be a full time musician."*

Who will be the next CEO? This person must have earned the trust of non-family employees, suppliers, customers, the family and shareholders. Most of these CEOs have been highly educated through college, industry sponsored programs, management certificates, and business schools. The CEO candidates past performance and ability to influence others are key indicators of their ability to lead. Ideally, they will understand and appreciate owner-manager relationships from the long-term continuity perspective.

One research study found that family businesses focusing on resilience and long-term sustainability outperformed non-family businesses focusing on short term financial performance.[11] This research also supported both La Tortilla Factory's and Lundberg Family Farms' values of being frugal, keeping the bar high for capital expenditure, and minimal debt.

They are likely to be more successful if the family CEO candidate has worked at another company for three to ten years before re-entry into the business. This experience brings a different perspective back to the business in terms of strategy, business models, and best business practices. It also builds the candidate's confidence and skill level in ways that is difficult to do within their own family.

Deciding on the next potential successor can take many years; it includes family discussions, an in-depth look at past performance, development of stretch assignments, and assessments. Successor candidates who are given feedback by their peers, supervisors, direct reports, customers, and family members, along with a commitment to changing behavior and developing themselves, will support a successful transition. The Board of Directors or a Committee of the Board will do the final review of successor performance and company strategy fit.

Some CEOs, Family Councils, and Boards of Directors form an independent advisory committee to guide the process of transition from one generation to the next. Non-family involvement brings objectivity to the process; the committee usually includes family members, key non-

---

11   Kachaner, N., Stalk, G. and Bloch, A., *What You Can Learn From Family Business: Focus on resilience, not short-term performance*. Harvard Business Review, November 2012.

family managers, estate attorneys, CPAs, and business planning advisors. This committee will bolster confidence and goodwill by leading a process that is thorough, transparent, fair, and thoughtful. Understanding, agreeing on, and following this process of selection will lead to the successful appointment of the next CEO.

Who else is a key figure in the transition from one generation to the next? While they rarely receive acknowledgement, the CEO's spouse is a central influence in business sustainability. The CEO's spouse is frequently very invested in the continuity and legacy of the business, thinking about the mutual benefit between the business, her children, nieces, and nephews. The spouse is often the person who acts as the family's beacon of trust, communication, and harmony. Spouses can either help or hinder the relationship between the family and the management of the business, shareholders, and extended family.

One of his or her most critical roles is acting as a daily coach to the CEO—listening and reflecting on business practices and decisions. An interested and mature spouse will see themselves as the steward of the family legacy and frequently the holder of the vision and mission. They may act as an ambassador of the business in the local community—delivering the company's message, serving in charitable organizations, and being an industry spokesperson. This is not to imply they are all angels—some spouses pit relatives against each other, protect their children's place in the company at the expense of the business, and demand more money than the business can afford. As juicy as this sounds, I believe it is the rare exception.

Industry, Diversity, and Growth

Aside from knowing the next CEO, the ability to build or acquire product and service diversity is crucial for sustainability. Providing for this growth rests heavily on the trust between family and key non-family managers. Not only will these managers need to be motivated to sustain company growth, but also their willingness and ability to coach and mentor the next generation is critical.

The current industry and financial environment involves frequent and rapid changes in business models, including globalization, an ever increasing use of technology, the structure of the value chain, and intensifying competition. Visionary but hard-working, competent family CEO leaders, their executive management team, and their Board of Directors are faced with an ongoing restructuring of business. The next generation will hopefully improve upon the previous generation. If well educated in the industry and in best business practices, they are more likely to engage in the strategic planning, information system implementation, financial system redesign, and e-commerce opportunities than their parents, aunts, and uncles. As the family grows, some businesses create a structure where each sibling branch runs a division, with separate shareholder agreements and wealth transition plans reflecting that sibling's controlling interest in their division.

Family Wealth Transfer and Liquidity Options

Estate planning, ownership transition planning, and liquidity options are necessary. In plain English, this is about planning on the transfer of your assets to your heirs with minimal tax consequences, transferring the ownership of the company to the next generation, and providing ways for heirs to "cash in" on their inherited assets if they choose to be out of the business.

Yes, we started the conversation about estate planning in Chapter 4, but it pops up again here because its absence can quickly destroy the business and family relationships. Family wealth, family relationships, and business sustainability will be supported with early, ongoing estate planning *and* the ability for family members to reasonably tap into their wealth. This planning is often avoided or simply ignored. When the planning does occur, it is frequently done with advisors who do not understand the full implications of the planning on finances, taxes, business continuity, business management, and family relationships.

My experience is that many CEOs tip-toe around the process because they fear that difficult conversations may erupt into conflict. Some plan, but don't involve other family members. Often, people avoid talking about wills and estate planning because it forces them to face their mortality. Creating a will, and deciding on the next CEO, signals to the person and everyone else that death is looming.

Often, acknowledging that your physical and mental capacities are diminishing is followed with a wave of self reflections and a critical look back at your accomplishments and failures. One client noted

"....it wasn't a wave; it was a tsunami—I am proud of the company's accomplishments but am now daring myself to look at the destruction I caused through two marriages and four children. All of that and I'm still not sure if there is enough left for my retirement, or if I've picked the right daughter to move into the CEO spot."

To top this all off, estate planning is time intensive, expensive, and confusing. You need to find out if family members want to be involved in the transfer of the business. Has one sibling poured themselves into the business and wants you to ensure that they have the voting power over their non-working siblings? Do you have the assets to "make it equal," fund your own retirement, and protect your spouse? Is your financial planner bugging you about having most of your retirement tied up in your business? It may be your sole source of cash flow. Where do you turn?

These are valid, heart wrenching questions. You are not alone. Many business owners have a majority of their wealth tied up in the business. Transferring equity may mean the transfer of current and future cash flow, as well as the transition of corporate control to the next generation.

You've likely heard from other owners that you should look at a Grantor Retained Annuity Trust (GRAT) or an Intentionally Defective Grantor Trust (IDGT). How do you go about deciding what will work best for you? Owners commonly choose one type of trust, run it by their accountant and tax attorney, and consider the planning done.

Owners who have been able and willing to do consistent retirement planning separate from the business equity are in a better position to transfer control in a timely manner, and thus support management's focus on business longevity instead of short term financial performance.

Let's face it…if you delay planning you don't have to let go of the control of the company—the very control that has brought success, advantage, esteem, and autonomy. While there are ways to control management of the business, such as through recapitalizing stock into voting and non-voting, there is a transition in front of you, decisions to be made, and no crystal ball. Are your children ready? Are you ready?

Transfer across generations requires an understanding of the following:

1. Financial retirement needs of the CEO and spouse

2. Ownership successor development

3. Retention of key non-family member leaders/managers

4. Strategic and capital needs of the business versus financial needs of the estate

5. Corporate governance and voting control in the next generation

6. Needs, motives, and intentions of each inheriting shareholder

7. Next generation expectations of the business

8. Abilities of the next generation as shareholders, members of a governing board, business managers, and leaders

9. Desire of family members not active in the management of the business to support business sustainability, which may require a decrease in dividends and capital investment

10. Liquidity needs of inactive or minority shareholders

11. Charitable intention of owners

12. Overall family relationships

Once you clearly understand what everyone wants and what you want for the business, then you are ready to sit down with your business planner, estate attorney, CPA, and tax attorney to discuss what options best fit. It is easy to see that succession and continuity planning is an intellectually and emotionally challenging process requiring advanced planning and a team of experienced professionals.

A comprehensive estate plan needs to address the allocation of income sources to the founder and his or her spouse, non-active family shareholders, and the inheritance or beneficial equity interest of the heirs. It should also address financial control of the company with buy-sell agreements, an agreement of how voting and non-voting stock is transferred, and the allocation of stock to qualified heirs. While the founding CEO and his or her spouse have the best intentions, distributing the voting shares equally among shareholders or creating a consensus-dependent, co-presidency between two siblings can spell disaster. Placing stock in complicated trust structures can also bite you down the road.

Helping everyone understand the difference between ownership as inherited and authority as developed is tricky. The next generation family leadership needs to have earned the trust and followership of key company stakeholders, both family and non-family. On the other hand, if stock ownership transfer is not made thinking about corporate control, it makes it more difficult for the next CEO to retain the authority to lead. This next generation of leaders needs to be able to lead from direct control or by being influential with siblings and cousins, as if they have a 51 percent voting control. If the current CEO withholds the authority to lead—by not transferring voting stock or by requiring next-generation shareholders to reach consensus on decisions—it will likely put company legacy at jeopardy. At best, it will take away the business's edge of being quickly decisive and agile against outside competition. It can also lead to conflict if the next generation, prospective CEO becomes tired of waiting and either retires early or migrates to a competitor.

One way to increase sustainability is to recapitalize common stock into two classes (voting and non-voting), thus allowing the previous generation to divide their estate equally among their heirs in terms of value, but differently in terms of corporate governance. Preferred stock recapitalization allows the value of ownership by the senior generation to be frozen with future growth of the business retained for the heirs.

A buy-sell agreement is frequently the vehicle for family shareholders to have the company stock realize value. Buy-sell agreements or stock purchase agreements typically include a right of first refusal provision with stock being first offered to the company or another family member. This agreement allows some family members to support the legacy of the family business while others can access needed cash. Again, Family Council meetings are a good venue for reviewing buy-sell agreements, stock purchase agreements, business valuations, and family loan programs.

Valuation approaches are varied and complex. They include an accounting approach (book value); market approach (comparison of companies within the same industry, multiple sales, multiple of earnings, multiple of equity); income approach (net present value of future benefits, net present value of cash flows or capitalization of earnings capacity, net present value of expected dividends); and cost approach (appraisal of tangible and intangible assets). As you can see, there are many approaches, and both professional and lay opinions vary as to which is the most fair. Generally speaking, an in-depth dialogue with shareholders, business leadership, a CPA, business planner, and valuation experts will clarify this decision.

How can you transfer wealth to the next generation? Will you gift and/or sell? How, other than a sale of stock, can you create liquidity? One option is to create an employee stock ownership program (ESOP), which can be a good tax strategy, create liquidity, and diversify your portfolio. If properly implemented, an ESOP can bring value to both the owner and employee.

Think you're done? Estate wealth transition, liquidity options, financial plans, and business governance planning is a multi-year process. When "complete," it is wise to do a periodic review to ensure that the plan is still in alignment with current tax codes and family intentions.

La Tortilla Factory

Carlos was thoughtful and consensus driven in his approach to the transition from himself to the next Chief Executive Officer. He encouraged objectivity by informing the Board of Directors, the family, their VP of Operations and Human Resources Jonna Greene, key non-family employees, and an external succession specialist. The succession from Carlos to their long-term Chief Financial Officer, Stan Mead, came at a time of anticipated growth that needed the guidance of someone who understood the industry, as well as the family. Stan was able to fill that role.

During the Chief Executive Officer transition, Carlos transitioned himself to Chairman of the Board and proceeded to add two non-family industry experts. The role and professionalism of the board gained traction and provided valuable guidance to the CEO and executive management team.

Carlos' estate planning and liquidity option planning for family members has been both structured and unstructured. As a result, he kicks himself for some of the lack of planning that has financially impacted the company and family. However, this pattern of on-and-off planning is common and points to the need for ongoing review.

For example, when Mike, his younger brother, decided to leave the company they once again reviewed and tightened up the buy-sell agreement; when Carlos and his brother Willie transitioned out of active company management to leadership positions on the Board of Directors, they jointly began looking at their individual financial plans along with options for wealth transfer of their company assets. This planning is continuous and disciplined, and any level of procrastination, along with changes in tax codes, can trigger another review and revision. Carlos has led the way for the next generation to become even more highly structured in their planning for business sustainability and family wealth transfer.

Lundberg Family Farms

Grant is a planner, as were his uncles and grandfather before him. They planned the planting and harvesting of fields, the marketing, and sale of their rice; they kept on planning for the transition from one generation to the next. When Eldon, Grant's father, relinquished control, he literally walked out of the company for a long vacation after announcing his belief in the next generation's ability to take the reins. One word that bubbles up in many of their conversations is "conservative," which goes hand in hand with "planning."

Business sustainability and family harmony are actively discussed at Lundberg Family Farms. This has driven them to the current state of structure that includes a buy-sell agreement, stock purchase agreement, business valuation process, business strategic plan, gifting and stock sale completion down to the third generation, most family members with comprehensive estate plans, and many with individual financial plans; all of this and a few of the fourth generation members are now working in the business. It is complicated considering the farm land is one entity and the company, Lundberg Family Farms, is another, with separate planning and governance for both.

Planning for sustainability is encouraged; the third generation has been granted planning assistance with access to an estate planning attorney. The business is aware that this planning will not only benefit the individual family member, but will also support long-term business sustainability.

The business planning has included being open to family members and non-family employees with ideas on how to diversify and expand product lines to accommodate a growing family and business that wishes to remain competitive and influential in their care of the land. From family wealth transfer planning to strategic planning, Lundberg Family Farms has actively worked at finding a balance between individual needs and business sustainability.

Interiors Unlimited

Planning at Interiors Unlimited was dominated by the adage that Neal liked to repeat: "It's my way or the highway." Business planning and family wealth transition were kept in Neal's head and minimally shared with his spouse, but not the rest of the family.

Growing the business to expand and provide opportunities for other family members was also not on the top of Neal's list. When Tom came to him to add a lucrative product line that was in alignment with their mission and other products, Neal refused to consider it because it wasn't his idea. Eventually, the market competitive pressures and business opportunity outweighed Neal's negativity, and Tom moved forward despite his father's veto. The product became one of their most profitable lines and they became the sole distributor in California and Arizona.

While planning was just one of the pieces that brought Interiors Unlimited to ruin, it was an important missing link. Neal's unwillingness to plan for wealth and business transition frustrated his son to the point of nearly destroying the business—and it did destroy their relationship. Tom laughed when asked if he ever sees himself sitting at the family Thanksgiving table with his father. His reply: "That's not happening—ever."

*   *   *   *   *

Business sustainability begs you to carefully prepare the next CEO, transition family wealth, and reexamine your business model. It is a process that is tricky, complicated, and sensitive. It requires consideration of the current and next generation financial and business control needs while tax considerations, liquidity needs, business sustainability, and differing emotional perspectives are juggled. Layer that with the cost of planning, finding the right advisors, gathering documents, as well as unsettling family discussions, and underlying thoughts of our own mortality, and it's easy to see why this is a necessary, but bumpy journey. It requires commitment, discipline, and emotional intelligence—grab a seat and hold on!

Questions for Chapter 8 – Building Business Sustainability:

1. What is your process for choosing the next CEO? Other key positions in the company?

2. Who is or isn't being prepared for company leadership?

3. If you are the CEO, how are you positioned to let go of day-to-

day operations?

4. How would you describe your financial preparation for retirement? What are you planning to do during retirement?

5. Is your current business model still relevant?

6. What have you tried for product and service expansion of the business?

7. What processes do you have in place to encourage business growth and diversity?

8. How do you know what next generation family members want from the business?

9. How would you describe the commitment of the current and next generation to keep the business within the family?

"Plan specifically so you can implement flexibility."

–DALLIN H. OAKS

CHAPTER 9

THE SLOW BAKE:
PREPARING THE NEXT GENERATION

Educating the Next Generation

An educated and knowledgeable next generation will drive business growth, bringing confidence, innovation, and energy into the workplace. So, who's ready? Who has the education, drive, and interpersonal skills to work or lead? This is an ongoing activity that includes supporting the formal education of individuals to increase their knowledge about the industry and your particular business. It includes learning about best business practices and how to care for the business.

Some families form scholarship programs to entice the next generation to come back into the family business; others educate simply because of the value they place on education. Be careful about insisting on specific degrees, as it may set someone up to choose an academic area where they have little interest or ability in order to receive the scholarship. Ideally, the review of the education policy will be followed by in-depth conversations and flexibility in order to meet the needs of the business and the individual.

To avert misunderstandings and resentments, provide everyone with a written education policy and be consistent in implementing it. Creating an education policy is simple when you are clear about the family's philosophy on higher education. For example, if you value higher education for its own sake, and you are willing to give scholarships of $10,000 a year for four years with no pay back or expectation of entry in the family business, your policy is written. If you expect them to get a degree in an area that will match the business need with a requirement of working in the business for three years, there's your policy.

Communicating the business's need for educated talent should be repeated many times as the next generation matures. Listing the business's current job education requirements and presenting those in a Family Council meeting for children as young as seven to ten will stimulate thinking about their interests and abilities. One teen, during a Family Council meeting, noted that "I know I'm going to major in music, but I'm glad I have heard about Uncle Joe's business....I'm now considering a minor in business, specifically in e-commerce, because of what I heard this weekend."

Education assistance need not be limited to college. It can be a technical institute or apprenticeship in a trade. One of my clients has several manufacturing facilities and a consistently understaffed mechanics department. In the third generation, there were several teenagers who loved working on their cars. At Grandpa's urging, they attended a technical institute and returned to work at the family business.

Explore several ways to embed industry knowledge into the family knowledge bank. The next generation can learn about the industry by attending trade shows with their parents, aunts, or uncles. Family Council meetings can include industry trends, patterns, and competitor data; distribute online subscriptions to industry magazines and newsletters. Give a team of the youngest generation a new industry trend to research and report back at a Family Council meeting, Board of Directors meeting, and/or the company's executive management team meeting.

Involve children early and often. Understanding their particular family business is important. By the time it reaches the third or fourth generation, it is sometimes assumed that everyone understands the business, its history, and what it takes to lead and govern. While that is generally true for the first two generations when family members are working in the business and business dominates the dining room table conversation, this becomes less likely in generations three and four. To build that knowledge, Family Council meetings can include tours of new facilities, a company update from the CEO, a presentation about new product and service lines, and introduction to non-family employees. As the next generation matures, sharing the business strategic plan and financial statements will round out their education.

Matching Talents to Need – the Family and Business Map

As we saw in Chapter 5, one of the Family Council exercises included creating a family map with birthdates, interests, education, employment, and status (in family business, governance or not). Now, let's enlarge that map to wall hanging size, along with the business's organization chart so you can see what positions need to be filled, what skills are needed, and who might be available to enter the changing business. Who will own this ongoing tracking of family and business talent needs? Many family businesses have missed an opportunity to bring in a talented family member simply because the family member didn't understand that their skills were needed or that a position was open.

Family Employment Guideline through the Family Council

"But I want to be the Operations Director now!" CEOs are often asked, pushed, and wined and dined in order to bring in one of their siblings, cousins, or other relatives. This puts them in the very awkward position of aligning with either the family or the business. It's great when they are approached about an open position that can be filled by a family member who will bring value, is well prepared, and has the respect of the family. Unfortunately, the CEO is often faced with the no-win situation of having to protect the business and other employees against a family member who is not a match to the business need.

First you must be clear about what your family's philosophy is on employment. Many family businesses cite that part of the perks of owning their own business is their ability to hire family. It feels good to be able to offer employment to family and brings a sense of loyalty and camaraderie into the workplace that is desirable. Are you willing to hire any family member who wants employment, regardless of the current business need? All things being equal, between a non-family prospect and a family member, do you all agree to hire family? If the family member has high potential and experience, but there isn't a current position, do you bring them in to expand a product or service line? Must family members present their employment desires first through the Family Council and then the CEO, or do they go directly to Human Resources? As you can see, there are many questions to be answered before drawing up an effective Family Employment Guideline.

Many non-family managers are very cautious about employment in family owned companies because of past experiences working where family are given positions because of who they are instead of what they can offer. Letting prospective non-family managers know that the family has prepared a process for fairly introducing family members into employment will help attract and retain good employees. Typically, the second generation siblings will form the policy and pass it by the CEO and Chairman of the Board for comment before presenting it for approval to the Family Council.

A written Family Employment Guideline communicates greater clarity, transparency, and a sense of fair play among family members and non-family employees. Generally the first generation does not struggle with this as they are begging family members to help and accept minimal pay…the proverbial Tom Sawyer painting the white picket fence. As the business thrives into the second and third generation, it becomes imperative to answer the tough questions around introducing family into the company. Developing these written guidelines is the first step in averting touchy conversations about family entry.

These employment guidelines generally state the purpose, philosophy, and employment conditions for entry into the business. It clarifies that the family member needs to meet the same criteria as non-family applicants, that they will meet performance requirements, and that they will be compensated within the company guidelines. Some family businesses also require a family member to work outside of the family business for three to five years before entering. The guideline lets family know they must go through an application, interview, background screening, reference check, and drug screening, as the position requires.

Another way to be involved is for an individual family member, team, or one family branch to interact as their own separate legal entity— as subcontractors to the primary family business. There should be a subcontractor policy created to insure that the bidding process creates fairness for both family and non-family.

Internships

Internships, mentoring, and job shadowing can be excellent ways to bring the next generation into the business. It can be as simple as following an aunt or uncle for a few days to observe what they do in the business, all the way to a formal summer internship with substantial projects within different functional areas. As mentioned, Lundberg Family Farms has what they refer to as a Boot Camp for the fourth generation (G4) that is a long weekend during the summer where they get to know themselves, their cousins, and the business better. They have also established a summer long internship.

For Lundberg, generation three was instrumental in creating these programs, because when they came into the business they often felt like they were flailing around trying to figure out where they fit in. They recount stories of randomly entering meetings, unsure if they should be simply observing or contributing. They rotated through different departments, not clear about where they should be or what they should be doing. This lack of clarity led to instances of stepping on each other's toes.

Consider developing relationships with local noncompetitive businesses that reciprocate an internship program. In other words, you accept their adult children for the summer and they take on yours. In this way the next generation gains work experience in another family business and increases their chance of receiving objective feedback about their performance. Impartiality is difficult to come by when a parent, aunt, or uncle is involved. Your family interns then bring back best business practices and practical work experience to the business.

Eventually the number of family members seeking employment outstrips the business need. When this happens, you can encourage business incubators or start-ups by family members by offering seed money to develop a business plan and cover initial costs. This potential growth can include new lines of services, new products, product line extensions, new markets for existing products or services, exports, joint ventures, or strategic alliances. Establishing and communicating a process to encourage this entrepreneurial type model during Family Council meetings will increase the mindset of sustainability and legacy.

A word of caution: encouraging growth simply to support family employment should be avoided. Any growth opportunity should be supported by competitive and economic factors that create real customer and shareholder value.

Money Management

A missing component in many families is the ability of the next generation to understand money management—from their own personal budget to reading company financials. That's why money management is a key discipline, both for the exiting and the incoming generation.

If the exiting generation is not financially prepared for retirement, they will need to continue working. The next generation begins grumbling that the previous generation is "just there to pick up a paycheck," but are not really contributing. On the other hand, the incoming generation may not know how to create a department budget, read profit and loss statements, or manage their own household budget. The generation before them may be justly concerned about turning over company financial management to them. This is why everyone needs to understand basic business and personal finances, as well as the discipline to stick to a budget.

A focus on and commitment to a conservative balance of spending and saving will serve the individual, family, and business well. Understanding the family business's philosophy on debt, cash flow, and capital investment is important for the next generation to consider and weigh in on. Has the company philosophy on money management changed with the next generation? What will best support business legacy? What level of reinvestment into the business is desirable? How is that balanced with the provision of fair shareholder distributions?

These are important questions for the family and executive managers to consider. Ideally, these conversations will be compiled and documented as the company fiscal or money management philosophy that is broadly shared at the company executive and manager levels, the Board of Directors, and Family Council. This document should also be reviewed on an annual basis to reinforce and bring up potential shifts in thinking and practice.

In order to jumpstart individual family members' financial plans for retirement, some family businesses cover the cost of a Certified Financial Planner or firm to provide these services. Inside the company, this same offering may be made to executive management team members, both family and non-family, as a way to support executives in preparing for a timely departure at or before retirement age. Another support for managing toward a financial goal for retirement is a company policy clarifying a mandatory retirement age.

The founding owner is generally very careful with their money, understanding the balance of business debt, cash flow, and reinvestment. The tight cash flow in early years usually translates into owners having stretches of little to no salary draw while they pour money into the business. Older children of the owner will experience this cash crunch, but by the time the younger children reach adolescence, Dad may make up for the early lack of time and money by overindulging them with cars, extravagant vacations, and other things. An older sibling of one of my clients put it succinctly when she said,

> *"Dad wasn't conservative with money with me; he was cheap. With my younger brother, Jimmy, he was the ultimate Disney Dad. Anything Jimmy wanted, he got. Now I work hard at the company and pull long hours, while Jimmy thinks we owe him a job...a job he doesn't do well."*

Money is one of the most frequent points of conflict in a family. Where are the dividends? Is she making more money than I am? Why does he get to use the company credit card and I don't? Developing fair, clear policies and agreements around dividends, stock sale and purchase, use of company credit cards, and loans is necessary for individual financial health, business fiscal sustainability, and family peace.

Working on building pride and commitment to the family business will include stories about the time and financial sacrifices previous generations made to build the business. This, coupled with the parents' prudent money management practices, will support the development of the next generation's practices of saving and spending. It will encourage a sense of appreciation and responsibility instead of entitlement.

Through Family Council meetings, the next generation will understand the care for and transfer of family wealth. Family meetings can also be a time to talk about charitable giving: The Family Council can task the next generation with the family's charitable giving program, from deciding on how a minimal dollar amount will be distributed to local charitable organizations to managing a grant proposal process.

As the next generation goes through these presentations and conversations with their parents, aunts, uncles, cousins, and advisors, they will begin to understand that the business is not their personal bank account balance, but a responsibility requiring on-going care and attention.

There are several ways to build responsibility for sound money management. One way for young, next-generation members is for parents to give children their own expense account. Children can work with their parents to determine what they generally "spend" during the year on different categories: school clothes, entertainment, sports equipment, etc. You can gradually move them from a weekly allowance to a quarterly or annual amount so they begin to learn how to budget for needs, wants, and emergencies. Generally, this is started sometime around age seven to twelve years old, depending on the child. Warning: If your child blows their budget early in the agreed upon period, adding money to their account will teach them that they will be rescued. Be willing and committed to endure whining.

Both Lundberg Family Farms and La Tortilla Factory are conservative money managers. Tim Schultz, the Vice President of Planning and Development at Lundberg, and a brother-in-law in generation three, recalls a funny story about being frugal. The second generation had developed a fleet of equipment for the farm that had served them well, was seen as crucial to the success experienced to that point, and best of all, was fully paid for. The third generation saw benefits in newer equipment, including speed, precision, and availability of talent to operate and service the newer equipment. For years there were many discussions between the second and third generation about the advisability of updating the equipment and whether it could pencil out. Occasionally, those discussions became heated. Finally, the third generation resolved to test their theory of newer equipment enabling more efficient planting

The McCormick-Deering Farmall F30 tractor that the Lundberg family brought from Nebraska in 1937

by renting the equipment they were advocating. This "test" proved the theory, and the third generation is now refreshing their farm's equipment fleet on a steady basis.

La Tortilla Factory's original family leadership team, Carlos, Willie and Mike, all worked hard in the beginning years with minimal compensation. La Tortilla Factory has taken it a step further by actively supporting their employees to have sound money management practices. They offer Dave Ramsey's Financial Peace University program during work hours at no cost to the employee, with feedback about how it has had a positive impact on their personal lives.

Tom at Interiors Unlimited talks openly that his father was also typical, as a founding owner, in watching business expenses and being prudent in the fiscal management of the business. Where the stories of

Lundberg, Tamayo, and Smith diverge is that while the Lundberg and Tamayo family were prudent money managers to ensure family business legacy, Neal's focus on money was to satisfy his own retirement needs and desire for control.

Questions for Chapter 9 – The Slow Bake: Preparing the Next Generation:

1. How are you increasing the next generation's knowledge of the family business?

2. What value does the family place on education?

3. Does the family financially support the formal education of the next generation?

4. Does the business provide internships or mentoring of the next generation?

5. What is the basic philosophy of money management within the business?

6. What is the family's basic philosophy of money management?

7. Are you and your siblings financially planning for and financially prepared for retirement?

"All change is not growth; as all movement is not forward."
–ELLEN GLASGOW

CHAPTER 10

LEADING FROM THE CURRENT TO IDEAL

The Snapshot – Build Awareness of Where the Family and Business Stand

I t's time to take a look in the mirror. Where does your family business need to improve? Is it in the area of family health, business planning, family wealth transfer, talent development, or governance? If you have answered the questions at the end of each chapter, you are well on your way to assessing your strengths, weaknesses, and needs. You can also do this by engaging an objective outside advisor, or by utilizing an independent, non-family Board of Director member. You could also do a full company assessment, resulting in a prioritized checklist of recommendations.

You can get a broad look at your family and business needs by interviewing a diverse swath of family across generations. Additional information can be gathered by family and non-family employee surveys and focus groups. Reviewing company documents, such as organizational charts, job descriptions, financial statements, and management succession plans, will provide further perspective. Combining the gathered information from interviews, surveys, company documents, and focus groups should lead to a rich snapshot of the current state of both the family and the business.

For example, family focus group questions could include:

1. What top three values do you think we hold as a family?

2. Do we clearly communicate what is happening in the business to non-employee family members?

3. How would you describe our level of financial transparency?

4. How well do we communicate potential career paths to the family?

5. Describe the preparation and selection process you think we go through when choosing the next CEO of the business.

6. What do you think the two main responsibilities of the Board of Directors are?

7. Where are you in the process of planning for the transfer of family wealth to the next generation? (Sometimes commonly known as your estate plan.)

8. What is our general family philosophy of money management?

9. How understandable and fair do you think the stock purchase agreement is?

10. Have we given you enough liquidity options (ways to get your money out) so you don't feel stuck in ownership of the business?

11. Are most family members interested in maintaining the family business?

12. Would the family consider preparing the business for an eventual sale?

13. Is there a family story that you think is significant?

14. Please describe your perception of how effective the Family Council is.

15. How well do you think we get along as family members?

16. Do we have any sibling rivalries that are negatively impacting the business?

17. How have we addressed family secrets that have threatened the business?

18. Is there anything else you think we should understand or consider as we go through this data gathering process?

Anticipate that these focus groups will take a minimum of an hour and a half. And if more than ten questions are addressed, it is more effective to schedule two meetings.

Non-family and family employee focus group questions could include:

1. What core values do you think employees demonstrate in the business?

2. How has strategic planning been accomplished in the business?

3. How do employees align their performance goals to business strategic goals?

4. How does the company budget and track budget variances?

5. Describe how family and non-family employees work together. Are hiring, performance evaluation, compensation, and promotion practices fair between the groups?

6. What is your understanding of the role of the Board of Directors?

7. What is your understanding of the role of the Family Council?

8. What are the pluses and minuses of working in this family business?

9. What is your understanding of how the next CEO will be selected?

10. What is your understanding of how the next CEO is being prepared?

11. What stories are told to new employees to orient them to "the way things are done around here"?

12. Is there anything else you think we should understand?

Once you have gathered all of this information, use a team of family members, non-family employees, family employees, and outsiders to review the information, identify trends, and develop an initial list of recommendations. The outside help could include a business professor from a local university, your corporate legal counsel, a business consultant, an independent Board of Director member, or a family friend who understands both the business and the family. The result should describe the business and family strengths, weaknesses, opportunities, and threats to transitioning to the next generation. It will likely end with a list of priorities, action items, and initiatives to be implemented.

Families handle this assessment in different ways. It can be communicated to the company and family as: 1) A company assessment, 2) Part of the process of developing a management succession plan, and/ or 3) A way to improve the business for long-term sustainability. It is important to be clear about what information you need to gather and how the information will be used to in surveys, interviews, and focus groups. If the process is transparent and the resulting data widely distributed, the family and company will benefit. Broadly distributing the results and final report shows respect to participants and starts to build a sense of teamwork and collaboration for impending change.

One company I worked with presented their findings during a full staff meeting of 250 employees, followed by a webinar for remote employees the next day, a meeting for the Board of Directors the following week, and a meeting for the full family a month later. A few months later, when a project based on one of the business's weakness was introduced with a budget, everyone understood and was supportive.

You have a written snapshot of the current state of the business and the family—now what? Employees are frequently asked questions about what does and doesn't work in the workplace, and the information vaporizes into a corporate black hole. After a few experiences like this, people simply don't participate. Instead, they might knowingly throw the survey process by giving the same rating for all questions or mutely sitting in a focus group. You cannot control their experiences prior to entering your business, but once in your culture, you can demonstrate that their input is valued and acted on. While employees know that not all of their ideas will bubble to the top as an action item, understanding what did and why builds trust and engagement.

The Vision Statement:
Where You Want the Family and Business to Be

Earlier we talked about developing a Family Charter that describes what the family values, hopes for, and commits to doing in relation to the family business. Now we are going to develop a similar document for the business.

Using your snapshot, you now have the data to know where you are doing well and where you need shoring up. The question to answer is: Where do you want to be three to ten years from now? The great news is that you are headed into an area researchers identify as a strength of family businesses—the ability to be resilient and hold a long-term view. Business researchers Kachaner, Stalk, and Bloch studied 149 publicly traded family businesses and found:

> "...when we looked across business cycles from 1997 to 2009, we found that the average long-term financial performance was higher for family businesses than for non-family businesses in every country we examined. The simple conclusion we reached is that family businesses focus on resilience more than performance. They forgo the excess returns available during good times in order to increase their odds of survival during bad times. A CEO of a family-controlled firm may have financial incentives similar to those of chief executives of non-family firms, but the familial obligation he or she feels will lead to very different strategic choices."[12]

Gather a group of diverse perspectives—family, business, professional—to create a written vision of where the business is headed. This is not a laundry list of what you produce or do, but a broad picture of your long-term view of the business as a family legacy. One example is:

> We deeply believe in our products and the value they bring to individual users and to the environment. We are committed to on-going research and development to continue creating products that protect the environment and delight our customers. We establish

---

12   Kachaner, N., Stalk, G. and Bloch, A., *What You Can Learn From Family Business: Focus on resilience, not short-term performance*. Harvard Business Review, November 2002, pp 102-106

work environments that are nimble, respectful, and consensus-driven. We are disciplined, thoughtful, and open in our approach to new products, expansion, partnerships, and alliances. We honor and protect our family legacy by gathering frequently, discussing, and innovating. We value our employees by engaging them in the growth of the business, supporting their development, and rewarding them for their contribution. As we continue these practices, we will remain profitable, balancing family needs with business capital needs. We have a national reach, and intend to expand to Europe and Asia within the next five years.

This vision clearly communicates to family shareholders and employees what is important. Vision statements, while almost always longer than a mission statement, can also be as short as one or two sentences.

You do not need to go through the extensive process of creating a vision statement on an annual basis. Reviewing and reconfirming it once a year is important and sufficient, with an in-depth relook every three to five years. This process can be wrapped into the preparation of the annual strategic planning and budgeting process.

The vision of how to move into the future and the pathway to do so will change as societies, cultures, businesses, and families evolve. One example is Boeing's Vision Statement in 1950. Their goal was to "become the dominant player in commercial aircraft and bring the world into the jet age." Their current vision is: "People working together as one global enterprise for aerospace leadership." These ongoing external and internal changes require you to systematically ensure the vision of the business remains in alignment with the family, customer, and external market forces.

The Family Charter is to the family what the Vision Statement is to the business. It paints a picture of what the family values, how they interact, and what their vision is of themselves. It usually contains values, expected codes of conduct, and how the family agrees to interact with each other and the business. It sometimes includes specifics about the formation of the Family Council, Family Employment Guidelines, and how to handle conflict. Just as every business's vision statement is different, every family has a unique charter. The following example will give you an idea of what the charter can look like:

ABC Company Family Charter

Our Family Charter's purpose is to clarify the values our family holds; our interactions between family and business; how family members enter the business; how we communicate and proactively handle conflict; how leadership is determined; and what the role of the Family Council will be.

Values

Our family values honesty, thrift, and transparency. We support our country and actively practice our faith in God. We exemplify these values in everything that we do. We support the movement of honesty, thrift, and transparency from the family and into the business.

Family & Business Interaction

We receive company updates from the CEO at Family Council and shareholder meetings, as well as through the quarterly family newsletter. We understand that we will take our comments and suggestions to the Family Council leader and the Chairman of the Board, not directly to management or employees.

Family Employment

Family members are not guaranteed employment—they are encouraged to understand the talent needs of the business, proactively align their education with the business needs, and work outside of the family business before entering. The details have been documented in the Family Employment Guideline that was adopted by the Family Council and Board of Directors.

Communication & Conflict

We commit to frequent and open communication. We take advantage of opportunities, both formal and informal, to become more skilled at interpersonal communication. We have a specific, written Family Council policy on how to address conflict with an underlying philosophy of quickly and directly working with each other in a respectful manner.

Leadership Selection

The process of selecting the next CEO is clarified in the company's management succession plan. The basic premise is that the CEO, family or non-family, will have the experience, knowledge, skills, and abilities to lead the company forward. The person will understand the industry, have proven leadership ability, be decisive, collaborative, and a fit to the family culture.

Family Council

The Family Council was formed to ensure that the family stay informed about the business, have a place to offer insight and vision, preserve family business history, maintain family values, and gain an understanding of the responsibility of caring for the business. The Council will meet twice a year for company education and socializing.

You have your snapshot (the company and family assessment) of where you are and a vision of where you want to be (the company Vision Statement and Family Charter). Now let's bravely look at the bumps and warts that need attention.

Identify the Gap: Grandma's Dry Cornbread

Who is going to tell Grandma her cornbread is dry and that none of us love the Christmas fruitcake? Identifying the gap between where you are now and where you want to be can be an intellectually and emotionally tough task. In this process, you have identified your current state and your vision of the future. It's time to focus on the areas that will most likely bring you to your knees. It's time to figure out where your weaknesses, as a business and a family, are lurking—what are the two or three things you can do to strengthen your family and business.

Starting is key. The number and breadth of tasks can be overwhelming, so start with a few small wins before diving into complex initiatives, such as a full family wealth transfer plan. If governance is an identified gap between what you have now (the snapshot of inconsistent Board of Directors meetings), and where you want to be (Vision Statement of an effective Board of Directors), create a family member only Board of Directors before bringing in an outsider. Other small wins could be to create a limited, informal internship program for the next generation, and out of that experience, build a comprehensive internship program for family and non-family.

Another approach is to gather a diverse group of perspectives, again from family, non-family, management, BOD members, and professional outsiders, and dive into the recommendations that emerged from the company and family assessment. Post the Vision Statement, Family Charter, focus group, interview, and survey results around a meeting room and begin having a conversation about how to prioritize.

Do you need to further clarify the current state of the business and family? What are the gaps? Develop a list of what needs to be done to close them—a list for the family and one for the business. Then, considering the resources available, decide what is most important to do. What changes will result in the most positive long-term impact?

Closing the Gap

You now have the following:

1. Company documents, interview transcripts, survey results, and focus group results that spell out the strengths and weaknesses of the business and the family.

2. A written document (snapshot) compiling all of the data with identified patterns and initial recommendations—one for the family and one for the business.

3. Clarity about the current state of the family and the business from the snapshot.

4. Clarity about the future state of the business—your written Vision Statement of the future of your business.

5. Clarity about the future state and vision of the family—a written Family Charter.

6. A list of prioritized actions, initiatives, and projects that will close the gap between the current state and future state of the business and family.

Now, let's create an action plan for the business and for the family. What tasks, initiatives, or projects will you commit to? Who will be responsible for each action? When will it be started? When will it be completed? What are the deliverables that will let you know you have been successful?

Anything that is written and can be modified works; the primary thing is the discipline to systematically measure progress and make adjustments. Can some of the identified projects be added to an already established tracking system? For example, could the business goals be wrapped into the company strategic plan? Can the family track progress at one of their Family Council meetings? See the example below for a better idea of how to organize your action plan.

ACTION PLAN: Management Succession

Original: 10.23.2012
Revision:

Objective 1: Internship Program Development

Objective 1	Internship program development for the next generation(G4).
Objective 2:	Money management training for the current generation(G3).
Objective 3:	Develop liquidity options for family members.
Objective 4:	Review and communicate changes to the Stock Purchase Agreement.

Objective 1: Internship Program Development

Strategies	Responsible Person	Resources (working with)	Start Date	Due Date	Done	Deliverables	Comments / Status
1.1 Identify areas to address and develop the Standard Operating Procedures (SOP) for the business internship program for Generation 4(G4).	Sarah	Bill Joe	12.31.12	6.1.13		1. Family Internship Standard Operating Procedure approved by Family Council & Executive Management Team	
1.2 Communicate SOP to the third and fourth generation. Communicate SOP throughout the company.	Bill	Joe	5.1.13	7.15.13		1. Record of communication to G3, G4 and company employees	
1.3 Decide on departments with open projects/needs for internship program.	Craig	Sally	6.1.13	7.15.13		1. List of departments, projects, and initiatives that an intern could assist with	
1.4 Develop guidelines for entry into Internship program.	Sarah	Susan Kimberly	2.1.13	4.15.13		1. Program guidelines	
1.5 Identify initial round of eligible family members that meet internship entry guidelines.	Kimberly	Susan Katie	1.1.13	2.15.13		1. List of eligible participants	
1.6 Develop invitation to participate.	Karen	Kimberly	4.1.13	6.1.13		1. Invitation template for participation	
1.7 Prepare and schedule internship orientation.	Bill	Joe	4.15.13	6.1.13		1. Written internship orientation-training & assignment	

Here's the process in a nutshell:

	Family	Business
Step 1	Data gathering – family focus groups, survey & individual interviews	Data gathering – Business document review, employee survey, employee focus groups & key employee interviews
Step 2	Family Assessment	Company Assessment
Step 3	Family Charter	Vision Statement
Step 4	Strengths, Weaknesses, Opportunities & Threats (family)	Strengths, Weaknesses, Opportunities & Threats (business)
Step 5	Prioritized list of recommendations for the family	Prioritized list of recommendations for the business
Step 6	Match the recommendations for family and business to check for alignment, gaps, and overlaps	
Step 7	Develop Family Action Plan	Develop Business Action Plan
Step 8	Implement and Track Family Action Plan	Implement and Track Business Action Plan
Step 9	Evaluate Family Progress	Evaluate Business Progress

I didn't lay this out to make you cry (well, maybe a little). This demonstrates the need for thoughtful planning of the process before you begin. Who should be involved in each step? How will the process and results be communicated and to whom?

Don't freak out about the length of this process; few family businesses go through it entirely. You can shorten the family assessment to a few group meetings, combine the business assessment with strategic planning, or spread the steps of the process across a longer time period.

The last step is to ensure that, once the plans are implemented and tracking is in place, you set a time to evaluate overall progress. After a goal is accomplished, what has changed? Six months later, has the change held? Are there other areas the business and family should be addressing?

Let's look at how our families have juggled this work:

La Tortilla Factory

Carlos was a planner from the beginning. He helped his dad, Jose, look at the different options for a business and researched several possibilities. Carlos credits his banking background and his graduate degree from the Thunderbird Graduate School of International Management for helping him lay the groundwork for the discipline of building a solid business plan and periodically stopping to confirm the proposed model. The plan for the family component was more fluid. Brothers, spouses, and children moved in and out of the business based sometimes on the company's need, and other times on the family member's need.

They are beginning, in the third generation, to have structure, expectations, and clarity to support the thoughtful integration of family members into the business. For example, the buy-sell agreement has been reviewed and updated, and the Family Employment Guideline has been crafted, so that there is a clear expectation that family members will enter through the Human Resource department.

Lundberg Family Farms

Grant is following a legacy of planners and thinkers—when to plant rice, how much, what fields, what varieties, and how to protect the land. As the complexity of the family and business has grown, they have become disciplined in their processes. In the business this is seen as a structured and strategic Board of Directors, a clear organizational reporting structure, written standards and operating procedures, comprehensive strategic planning, and budgeting. In the family this has been accomplished with a formal summer internship, a Boot Camp experience for the fourth generation, Family Council meetings, and beginning coordinated estate planning.

Interiors Unlimited

Planning at both the business and family level was started, carried out and completed in Neal's head. There was no strategic planning process, but plenty of family shouting matches. Business planning was ad hoc on client acquisition and retention without product and service business models.

The uplifting end of this story is that Tom is quickly becoming successful in his business while improving his work-life balance. The family in the family business is now his wife, children, and hopefully, in the future, his grandchildren. Tom has been able to shift the culture of the workplace, create a successful business model, control finances, and bring in employees that support business growth.

Questions for Chapter 10 – Leading from the Current to the Ideal:

1. Do you have a written "snapshot" of the current health and well-being of the family?

2. Have you developed a written Family Charter?

3. Have you identified the gaps between the family "snapshot" and the Family Charter?

4. Do you have a plan to address the family gaps?

5. Do you have a written "snapshot" of the business?

6. Have you developed a Vision Statement for the business?

7. Have you identified the gaps between the business "snapshot" and the business Vision Statement?

8. Do you have a plan to address the business gaps?

"Other things may change us, but we start and end with family."

–ANTHONY BRANDT

CHAPTER 11

THANKSGIVING DINNER:
CELEBRATING AND
STRENGTHENING THE FAMILY

W e've covered a lot of ground. You've strengthened your family relationships, hired the talent the business needs, are developing the next CEO, have an effective Board of Directors, formed a Family Council, created an internship program for the next generation, developed a strategic business plan, and created a family wealth transition plan. When one of these areas seems complete, it's time to review and adjust. This treadmill of activity and emotion can quickly move from a feeling of slight tension to chronic anxiety with intermittent panic attacks. One way to decrease the pressure is to pause and celebrate success.

Celebrating Now

Owners and leaders find themselves over-the-top stressed trying to juggle family and a rapidly changing business environment. There is a fear that it will never end. When you get in that mode, you become counterproductive—obsessing about what has happened and might happen next. The present moment slips by unnoticed. Stopping to enjoy the "now" brings more joy into your life.

I know this is easier said than done. As I'm writing this, I'm looking out my front window at a beautiful pomegranate tree, a bed of irises, and a hummingbird feeder, wondering if I should have asked a different question of the CEO successor yesterday and worrying that I may not see my granddaughter this weekend. This is how our brain often diverts us. It takes discipline to stay in the now, yet it is a discipline that can bring a sense of contentment, accomplishment, and celebration to each moment. I have observed that effective leaders focus their full attention to the current task or decision in front of them. This frees them to ask great questions, sense what others are feeling, and find patterns in complex data.

Where is this leading? Being fully in the present moment allows you, as a family business leader, to decrease stress, accomplish more, and learn to notice small victories. You still want to actively plan for celebrations and family gatherings, but you don't need to wait for these events to discover and admire the "now." For example, the new inventory system is finally in place, and everyone is trained—now take time to notice the difference and thank those who made it possible.

When did you last take a vacation without the connection of a smart phone? Taking time to celebrate and strengthen includes individual time away to recharge yourself. I have heard and experienced all of the excuses and renditions of "I'm too busy." If you are not able, after the first three or four years of business start-up, to completely unplug and withdraw for at least a week, then you have not fully developed your team. Delegate, develop, cross-train, mentor, coach, and then find a remote beach with an umbrella drink.

Family Events & Celebrations

Family and business celebrations come in many forms. The Family Council can take on the task of ensuring that the family stays connected to each other and to the business. Some do this with e-newsletters, Facebook, scheduled family celebrations, or business events.

Events can be overwhelming, so be sure to spread out the work of the planning, set-up, and clean-up. Something as simple as meeting for a catered picnic at a local park, with each family responsible for bringing an outdoor game to share, can be as effective for strengthening the family as traveling to a destination vacation resort. Move the planning of these events around to different family teams and diversify team membership across family branches. The objective is to create a space for positive interaction on a regular basis.

Do not force interaction. Requiring participation may be possible if the "transfer of wealth" carrot is dangled, but it will taint the relationship. A forced gathering puts people on the defense, breaks trust, and builds resentment. Prepare by thinking about the different age groups that will be present, their interests, and how you can satisfy as many people as possible. Plan, invite, set-up, and release control. Accepting that you will not make everyone happy is a great life lesson.

What other celebrations can you plan as a family? Here are a few ideas:

- Center an event around food: Fix a meal together, or have a "progressive dinner," in which everyone drives from one house to the next for each portion of the meal.

- Craft something together: It can be anything from soaps to gingerbread houses to your own flavored olive oil.

- Get active: Hike, kayak, skydive, organize a soccer game, or attend a sporting event together.

- Create a family scavenger hunt: Find out unusual, obscure facts about your family members, write them down, throw them into a bag, shake them up, and then have your family take turns pulling out the facts and guessing who they are about. This game is a great way to get to know each other while having fun.

- Play board games: That's right, those old things that don't come with video graphics and sound. I attended a family gathering that had eight games of Pictionary going on at once, laughter filled the home.

- Have a talent show: People can sing, dance, tell a story, play an instrument, act, bring their art work, juggle, or do magic.

Preparation is key—giving out simple rules on the length of time and types of talent demonstrations will increase success. Add a bit of competition with a panel of judges and prizes.

- Take a walk down memory lane: Create a family album or video with photos, stories, and memorabilia. Split into teams of three, create a page, piece it together, reproduce it, and give to all family members.

- Volunteer together: Build a home with Habitat for Humanity, participate in a walk to raise money for a favorite charity, distribute food at your local food bank, or clean up a local river or park.

- Be creative: You can expand beyond the "just have fun" concept to create interactions which build in-depth relationships. Families can talk about how they both positively and negatively handle stress and anxiety. They can identify their communication and interaction patterns—what works and what doesn't. The family can gather in a circle and say one thing they appreciate about each other or one thing about their family that they are thankful for. The possibilities are endless.

Business Interactions and Celebrations

"The only rock I know that stays steady, the only institution
I know that works, is family."

−LEE IACOCCA

Send a team of family members who don't work in the business to the annual industry tradeshow. They will learn about the industry and competitors while connecting with family and non-family employees. Ask these same family members to join your employees for the monthly birthday celebration at the company or to the annual all-staff meeting. Like any relationship, more interaction leads to a deeper understanding, and hopefully a growing respect for each other.

At La Tortilla Factory, it is common to see Willie or Carlos leading a group of visitors on a tour of their tortilla manufacturing floor—these interactions are, in and of themselves, a time for family leaders to step back and be satisfied with what they have accomplished. Grant and other family members also proudly show their state-of-the-art building in Richvale, California. Tom actively planned with others to create work spaces to support employees and respect their comfort.

Sharing and Preserving Family History

Sharing family history is powerful. Most of the stories we tell are about funny and meaningful interactions we have had. Children soak up stories about their relatives and beg for more. We listen, laugh, cry, and retell our favorites. I can remember moaning when my dad would pull out a slide carousel of pictures from family vacations, but ten minutes later I would be laughing with my brothers and sister.

How can you capture your family's history and the history of the family business? There are many creative ways like recording Grandpa telling his favorite stories about the early years of the company. Encourage a young relative to interview family and write a series of short stories. Give a project to the next generation that requires them to interview family and non-family members about the business's beginning, as well as important family events. The retelling of these stories will reveal family beliefs and values.

Artifacts in the business are important. Lundberg Family Farms integrated both the old and the new in their work spaces. Photos of the original family, a display of old manufacturing equipment, written value statements, and employee pictures remind our hearts and minds to pause and feel thankful. Pictures of their founding grandparents and the subsequent generation of the "four brothers" line the walls—togetherness, history, and legacy quietly affirm the importance of family and their love of the land.

La Tortilla Factory artifacts celebrate both their cultural and family heritage. The building colors, inside and out, are bright shades of yellow, orange, green, and red combined to honor their Mexican heritage. A quilt hanging in the lobby tells their family story. Pictures throughout the building reflect the importance of their business journey.

Interiors Unlimited looked like any other sterile corporate environment: sturdy gray carpet and flat white paint. Neal's office was at the very front. He had a large glass internal window so he could keep track of the front office and the involvement of the staff. Employees dubbed it the "command and control center." The staff lounge doubled as a conference room. There were no frills and no pictures other than a large oil portrait of Neal, which dominated his office. A small drafting room was barely visible from the staff lounge—an inadequate space where the bulk of their work was done. Tom, Neal's son, moved from that building and created his own space. The office is open, the energy high, and smiles plentiful. The work space for the drafters and estimators is large and was designed to encourage simultaneous viewing of blueprints, support innovation with technology, and allows room to gather for collaboration.

Questions for Chapter 11 – Thanksgiving Dinner: Celebrating and Strengthening the Family:

1. What family events do you celebrate?

2. What business events and celebrations have worked well?

3. How does your workplace reflect a celebration of the success of family and business?

4. What successes could you place more focus on?

5. What small wins, as a family and as a business, could you pause to enjoy?

*   *   *   *   *

The Journey's End – Dessert Has Arrived

I am deeply honored when I am invited into a family business. Though my career has introduced me to some real characters, I always find them endearing (eventually). I mean, who knowingly exposes their family's personal dynamic to the level that families in business do? Who allows outsiders to comment on the errant communication patterns between their siblings? How dare I tell you that you need to plan more, sooner, when I am guilty of neglecting my own estate planning?

I have some quirky ways of communicating with one of my brothers, but if an outsider were so brazen as to point that out, I would definitely start plotting my revenge on them and anyone else who dared speak ill about my family relationships. How do you do it?! You are advised and sometimes emphatically told what to say, what to plan, how to talk to your sister, how to parent, how to manage money, and how to transfer leadership to the next generation. You digest this with a smile and often sizable outlay of cash. Then you turn around to try some of the advice, and wait for the family to react.

Yes, there are privileges and perks to owning a family business, including individual growth potential that will far outstrip most life experiences. Still, it can be heart wrenching and ultimately destructive if not thoughtfully approached. I trust that you have found a few new ideas that will give you tools to look deeper at your business and family.

You are braver than most.

I wish you, your family, and your business well.

ABOUT THE AUTHOR

Lois Lang, Psy.D., is a family business expert, author, and speaker. For nearly two decades she has assisted family business transitions by assessing the next generation's readiness, strengthening the executive team, and facilitating tough conversations. Her breadth of experience with over 200 different family-owned companies gives her a unique vantage point that supports her work of helping family businesses move to the next level of performance.

Lois is also a founding partner of Evolve Partner Group, LLC with offices in Seattle, Washington and Stockton, California. While her focus is on family business, Evolve Partner Group offers management succession services to a wide range of industries. They facilitate the strengthening of teams, sync business strategies with transition planning, and optimize succession outcomes. They also create customized transition plans that align talent, planning, and business processes.

Lois began her career as a nurse administrator in hospital systems on the East Coast. She then became the Director of Organizational Development for Families First, the largest non-profit foster care entity in California. Since 1998, she has consulted businesses and non-profits around talent development, management succession, team development, and leadership.

Lois received a Masters in Public Administration/Healthcare Services from the University of San Francisco and a doctorate in Industrial-Organizational Psychology from The Professional School of Psychology in Sacramento. Her academic work focused on organizational culture change and neuroscience. Her background and education in culture change management, executive coaching, strategy, and relationship development bring value to family business clients.

LOIS LANG CAN HELP YOUR FAMILY BUSINESS PROSPER

Lois Lang helps family businesses work through a variety of growth and transition hurdles. Family business leaders commonly call on her to assist in the following areas:

- **Develop the current leadership team and next generation through executive coaching.** If you want strong talent that can support and sustain the company, coaching your prospective and current leaders is a must. Lois' executive coaching is based on neuroscience principles, coupled with setting and tracking individualized skill and behavioral goals. As a coach, Lois builds trust, listens, makes observations, points out reality, stimulates deeper thought by questioning, and then holds the individual accountable to changes they commit themselves to do.

- **Lead families through the difficult conversations that occur when running a business with relatives.** Many crucial decisions are delayed as family members either avoid the dreaded conflict of the discussion or charge into a loaded conversation that quickly deteriorates into a yelling match. Lois brings objective insight and facilitation skills that gently peel back the layers of individual motives and interests to bring the family to a deeper understanding and an ultimate decision that is a win-win for the business and family.

- **Utilize your professional team.** Lois helps you orchestrate the team of advisors you will need during any succession or transition issue, including your accountant, certified financial planner, business consultant, valuation expert, and attorney. Lois helps you utilize and coordinate the professional team to ensure that all of your bases are covered, business risk is mitigated, and the family understands the dance of trusted advisors.

With Lois on your side, you can strengthen the business, build family harmony, and create a family-owned company that lasts for generations to come.

LOOK WHAT LOIS' CLIENTS HAVE TO SAY...

"As owners of a vineyard and winery, we were always on the move and not sure if we were preparing the business for our son and daughter. Lois has helped us form a Board of Directors and Family Council, as well as embrace a non-family general manager. We can honestly say we completely relaxed on our last vacation, knowing that the business was moving in the right direction without our constant help!"

— Fred and Sally Schweiger, Schweiger Vineyards

"Lois has helped our family business integrate the next generation into the business, develop our Family Council, and make the leadership transition from the last non-family CEO back to a family member."

— Jeff Veilleux, CEO, PJ's Rebar, Inc.

"Lois has assisted our family through some delicate conversations with the transition from my mother as leader to me. The combination of family meetings, individual coaching sessions, and communication training has helped us learn how to lead as a family, and has supported the growth of the Inn."

— Cally Dym, Inn Manager, Little River Inn

LOIS LANG WILL INSPIRE AND EDUCATE YOUR TEAM

Lois Lang is an engaging, interactive, and motivational speaker. By coupling solid wisdom with real-life stories, she shares the keys to unlocking the next level of performance in your family business. Her primary speaking topics include:

- **Preparing the Next Generation in a Family Business:** Learn how to increase the leadership and management skills of family currently in the business, as well as the skills of family shareholders who do not work in the company. In this session, Lois helps everyone become aware of their roles and responsibilities, which enables the family business to succeed.

- **Best Practices in Family Business Governance:** Are you using your Board of Directors, Family Council, Family Foundation, and/or Family Office the right way? Do you even have all these things? Now you can gain clarity about the roles and responsibilities of each family and non-family member in a governance position in order to decrease anxiety and increase effective decision-making.

- **Culture Change:** Organizational culture is simply defined as "the way we do things around here." What's your business' culture and is it effective for long-term success? Have Lois guide you and your team through a process of defining your current culture and its fit to the desired work environment.

- **Management Succession:** Is your next generation ready to take the reins? Without a detailed transition plan, both the current and next generation will face hurdles that can disrupt operations. In this eye-opening presentation, Lois inspires you and your team to take the steps necessary to ensure business continuity.

- **Leadership Skill Development:** Strong, active leadership by the management team is vital for company growth and sustainability. In this dynamic presentation, Lois leads attendees to the awareness and motivation they need to embark on a personal growth process. She then shares key leadership competency insights on organizational culture, change management, advanced communications skills, and effective performance management that will propel your business forward.

LOOK WHAT OTHERS HAVE SAID ABOUT LOIS' SPEAKING PRESENTATIONS:

"Lois was very engaging—the exercises were great learning tools."

"What I found most useful was seeing in myself what I needed to improve by working with my group in the exercises."

"The breakout communication exercises were great, especially with Lois going from group to group listening and providing useful insight."

"Very good presentation. It brought concepts and applied them to real world issues. This course (performance evaluation training) should be mandatory for all management."

CONTACT LOIS AT:
lois.lang@evolvepartnergroup.com
www.evolvepartnergroup.com
209.952.1143